ISBN 978-1-292-13244-0

High-frequency words

porter	to wear
poser	to place
pousser	to push
préférer	to prefer
présenter	to introduce (a person), to present
prêter	to lend
se promener	to go for a walk
quitter	to leave (somewhere, somebody)

Had a look ☐ **Nearly there** ☐ **Nailed it** ☐

raconter	to tell, to recount
se rappeler	to remember
rater	to fail, to miss (train, bus, etc.)
rechercher	to research
recommander	to recommend
regretter	to regret, to be sorry
rembourser	to refund
remercier	to thank
remplacer	to replace
rencontrer	to meet
rentrer (à la maison)	to return (home), to go back (home)
renverser	to knock over
réparer	to repair
répéter	to repeat
se reposer	to rest
réserver	to reserve
ressembler	to look like, to resemble
rester	to stay
retourner (à l'école)	to return (to school), to go back (to school)
se réveiller	to wake up
rouler	to go (in a car)

Had a look ☐ **Nearly there** ☐ **Nailed it** ☐

sauter	to jump
sauver	to save
sembler	to seem
signer	to sign
signifier	to mean, to signify
sonner	to ring (a bell)
souhaiter	to wish
stationner	to park
téléphoner	to phone
(se) terminer	to end
tirer	to pull
tomber	to fall
toucher	to touch

travailler	to work
traverser	to cross, to go across
trouver	to find
utiliser	to use
vérifier	to check
voler	to fly, to steal
voyager	to travel

Had a look ☐ **Nearly there** ☐ **Nailed it** ☐

Common –ir verbs

atterrir	to land
choisir	to choose
s'endormir	to fall asleep
finir	to finish, to end
nourrir	to feed, to nourish
offrir	to offer, to give a present/gift
ouvrir	to open
partir	to leave, to depart
prévenir	to warn
remplir	to fill, to fill in
réussir	to succeed
se servir de	to use
sortir	to go out
se souvenir	to remember
tenir	to hold
venir	to come

Had a look ☐ **Nearly there** ☐ **Nailed it** ☐

Common –re verbs

apprendre	to learn
attendre	to wait for
boire	to drink
conduire	to drive
connaître	to know (person, place)
décrire	to describe
descendre (de)	to get out of (bus, car, train)
dire	to tell, to say
entendre	to hear
éteindre	to switch off
(se) faire mal	to hurt (oneself)
introduire	to introduce (an item, an idea)
lire	to read

Had a look ☐ **Nearly there** ☐ **Nailed it** ☐

mettre	to put
plaire (à)	to please
prendre	to take
produire	to produce

High-frequency words

remettre	to put back
répondre	to reply
rire	to laugh
sourire	to smile
suivre	to follow
vivre	to live
vendre	to sell

Had a look ☐   Nearly there ☐   Nailed it ☐

Common –oir verbs

avoir	to have
avoir besoin de	to need
avoir l'intention de (faire)	to mean to (do)
devoir	to have to, must
savoir	to know (a fact)
voir	to see
vouloir	to want

Had a look ☐   Nearly there ☐   Nailed it ☐

Common adjectives: describing someone

actif/-ve	active
agréable	pleasant
amical(e)	friendly
bavard(e)	talkative
bête	silly
calme	peaceful, quiet, calm
désagréable	unpleasant
drôle	funny (comical)
égoïste	selfish
généreux/-euse	generous
gentil(le)	kind
gros(se)	fat
honnête	honest
indépendant(e)	independent
intelligent(e)	intelligent, clever
joli(e)	pretty
laid(e)	ugly
marrant(e)	funny (comical)
méchant(e)	naughty
mince	slim

Had a look ☐   Nearly there ☐   Nailed it ☐

moche	ugly
mûr(e)	mature
optimiste	optimistic
paresseux/-euse	lazy
(im)patient(e)	(im)patient
pessimiste	pessimistic
petit(e)	small, short (person)

(im)poli(e)	(im)polite
populaire	popular
responsable	responsible
rigolo(te)	funny (comical)
sage	good (well-behaved), wise
sérieux/-euse	serious
sévère	strict
strict(e)	strict
sympa (invariable)	nice, likeable
sympathique	nice, likeable
timide	shy
travailleur/-euse	hard-working
vilain(e)	naughty

Had a look ☐   Nearly there ☐   Nailed it ☐

Common adjectives: I am, you are, we are …

célèbre	famous
content(e)	pleased
de bonne humeur	in a good mood
étonné(e)	surprised
faible (en maths, etc.)	weak (in maths, etc.)
fatigué(e)	tired
fort(e) (en maths, etc.)	strong (in maths, etc.)
heureux/-euse	happy, content
inquiet/-iète	worried
jeune	young
malheureux/-euse	unhappy
perdu(e)	lost
pressé(e)	in a hurry
reconnaissant(e)	grateful
riche	rich
satisfait(e)	satisfied
sauf/-ve	safe
surpris(e)	surprised
triste	sad
vieux/vieil/vieille	old

Had a look ☐   Nearly there ☐   Nailed it ☐

Common adjectives: opinions

amusant(e)	fun, amusing
bruyant(e)	noisy
cher/-ère	expensive
chouette	great (fantastic)
démodé(e)	old fashioned
dur(e)	hard
effrayant(e)	frightening
facile	easy, simple
fantastique	fantastic
fatigant(e)	tiring
favori(te)	favourite
formidable	great (marvellous)

Contenu

High-frequency words **4**

Module 1
Words I should know for speaking and writing activities **15**
Extra words I should know for reading and listening activities **18**

Module 2
Words I should know for speaking and writing activities **19**
Extra words I should know for reading and listening activities **22**

Module 3
Words I should know for speaking and writing activities **23**
Extra words I should know for reading and listening activities **26**

Module 4
Words I should know for speaking and writing activities **27**
Extra words I should know for reading and listening activities **30**

Module 5
Words I should know for speaking and writing activities **31**
Extra words I should know for reading and listening activities **34**

Module 6
Words I should know for speaking and writing activities **35**
Extra words I should know for reading and listening activities **38**

Module 7
Words I should know for speaking and writing activities **39**
Extra words I should know for reading and listening activities **42**

Module 8
Words I should know for speaking and writing activities **43**
Extra words I should know for reading and listening activities **46**

High-frequency words

Common –er verbs

accepter	to accept
adorer	to love, to adore
aider	to help
aimer	to like
aller	to go
aller à pied	to walk
allumer	to light, to turn, to switch on
améliorer	to improve
(s')arrêter	to stop

Had a look ☐ Nearly there ☐ Nailed it ☐

chanter	to sing
chercher	to look for
cliquer	to click (ICT)
coller	to stick
commander	to order
compter/compter sur	to count, to intend, to count on (someone)
contacter	to contact
continuer	to continue, to carry on
copier	to copy
se coucher	to go to bed
coûter	to cost

Had a look ☐ Nearly there ☐ Nailed it ☐

se débrouiller	to cope, to manage, to get by
décider	to decide
décoller	to take off (plane)
se dépêcher	to hurry
dépenser	to spend (money)
se déshabiller	to get undressed
désirer	to want, to desire
dessiner	to draw
détester	to hate
discuter	to discuss
donner	to give
durer	to last

Had a look ☐ Nearly there ☐ Nailed it ☐

s'échapper	to escape
écouter	to listen
écraser	to squash
empêcher	to prevent
endommager	to harm, to damage
entrer	to enter, to go in
envoyer	to send
espérer	to hope
essayer	to try
étudier	to study
expliquer	to explain

Had a look ☐ Nearly there ☐ Nailed it ☐

se fâcher	to get angry
fermer	to close, to switch off
frapper	to knock, to hit
gagner	to earn, to win
garder	to look after, to mind (child, dog)
garer	to park
gérer	to manage (business)
s'habiller	to get dressed
habiter	to live (inhabit)
informer	to inform
inviter	to invite
jeter	to throw

Had a look ☐ Nearly there ☐ Nailed it ☐

laisser	to leave behind (an object)
(se) laver	to wash
se lever	to get up
louer	to rent, to hire
manger	to eat
manquer	to miss, to be lacking
marcher	to walk, to work (function)
mériter	to deserve
monter	to climb, to get on(to), to go up
monter (dans)	to get into (bus, car, train)
montrer	to show
nettoyer	to clean
noter	to note

Had a look ☐ Nearly there ☐ Nailed it ☐

s'occuper de	to look after
organiser	to organise
ôter	to take off (clothes etc.)
oublier	to forget, to leave something behind
pardonner	to forgive
parler	to speak
passer	to pass, to spend (time)
penser	to think (about)
peser	to weigh
pleurer	to cry

High-frequency words

génial(e)	great (fantastic)
idéal(e)	ideal
incroyable	unbelievable
injuste	unfair
inutile	useless
juste	fair

Had a look ☐ Nearly there ☐ Nailed it ☐

magnifique	magnificent
malsain(e)	unhealthy
merveilleux/-euse	marvellous
nécessaire	necessary
négatif/-ve	negative
parfait(e)	perfect
passionnant(e)	exciting
positif/-ve	positive
pratique	practical
préféré(e)	favourite
raisonnable	reasonable
ridicule	ridiculous
sain(e)	healthy (food/way of life)
sensationnel(le)	sensational
sensass	sensational
simple	easy, simple
super	great (fantastic)
superbe	superb
utile	useful
valable	valid
vrai(e)	true

Other common adjectives

à la mode	fashionable
ancien(ne)	former, old
autre	other
chaud(e)	hot
court(e)	short
d'une grande valeur	valuable
dernier/-ière	last
étroit(e)	thin, narrow
fermé à clef	locked
grand(e)	large, big
gratuit(e)	free (at no cost)
grave	serious
gros(se)	large, big
haut(e)	high, tall (building)
léger/-ère	light
libre	free (unoccupied, available)
long(ue)	long
lourd(e)	heavy

Had a look ☐ Nearly there ☐ Nailed it ☐

même	same
moderne	modern
mouillé(e)	wet
mûr(e)	ripe
neuf/-ve	new (brand new)
nombreux/-euse	numerous
normal(e)	normal
nouveau/nouvel/nouvelle	new
ouvert(e)	open

Had a look ☐ Nearly there ☐ Nailed it ☐

pareil(le)	alike, the same
plein(e)	full
pourri(e)	rotten
prêt(e)	ready
prochain(e)	next
propre	own
rangé(e)	tidy
rapide	fast
récent(e)	recent
reconnu(e)	recognised, well known
réel(le)	real
silencieux/-ieuse	silent
situé(e)	situated
tranquille	peaceful, quiet, calm
type	typical

Had a look ☐ Nearly there ☐ Nailed it ☐

Comparisons/Superlatives

plus/moins	more/less
plus que/moins que	more than/less than
bon/meilleur/le meilleur	good/better/best
mauvais/pire/le pire	bad/worse/worst
bien/mieux/le mieux	well/better/best
mal/plus mal/le plus mal	badly/worse/worst
beaucoup/plus/le plus	a lot, lots/more/the most
peu/moins/le moins	few, little/less/the least

Had a look ☐ Nearly there ☐ Nailed it ☐

Common adverbs

à peine	hardly
assez	fairly, quite
aussi	too, as well
trop	too
bien	well
bientôt	soon
bon marché	cheap(ly)
d'habitude	usually
debout	standing

High-frequency words

déjà	already	au-dessus de	above
encore	again	autour de	around
ensemble	together	avant	before
fort	loud(ly)	avec	with
(mal)heureusement	(un)fortunately	chez	at (someone's house)
ici	here	contre	against
immédiatement	immediately	dans	in (inside)
jamais	never	de	from
là	there	dehors	outside
là-bas	over there		
là-haut	up there		
longtemps	(for) a long time		

Had a look ☐ Nearly there ☐ Nailed it ☐

		depuis	since, for
		derrière	behind
		devant	in front of, in the front
normalement	usually	en	in, within (time)
nulle part	nowhere	en dehors de	outside (of)
partout	everywhere	en face de	opposite
pas encore	not yet	en haut	above
peut-être	perhaps	en-dessous	under/underneath
plutôt	rather	entre	between
presque	almost	jusqu'à	until
quelque part	somewhere	loin de	far from
quelquefois	sometimes	malgré	despite, in spite of
rarement	rarely	nulle part	nowhere
récemment	recently	par	through
souvent	often	parmi	among(st)
surtout	especially	pour	for, in order to
toujours	always, still	près (de)	near (to)
tout de suite	straight away, immediately	sans	without
très	very	selon	according to
vite	quickly	sous	under/underneath
vraiment	really	sur	on (on top of)
		vers	towards

Had a look ☐ Nearly there ☐ Nailed it ☐

Had a look ☐ Nearly there ☐ Nailed it ☐

Prepositions

à	at, to
à côté de	next to
à partir de	from
à travers	across
après	after
au bord de	at the side/edge of
au bout de	at the end of
au fond	in the background, at the back
au fond de	at the back of, at the bottom of
au lieu de	instead of
au milieu (de)	in the middle (of)
au premier plan	in the foreground

Connectives

à cause de	because of
à part	apart from
ainsi	so, therefore
alors	so, therefore, then
aussi	also
car	because
cependant	however
c'est-à-dire	that is to say, i.e.
comme	as, like
d'un côté/de l'autre côté	on the one hand/on the other hand
donc	so, therefore

Had a look ☐ Nearly there ☐ Nailed it ☐

High-frequency words

ensuite	next	trente	30
évidemment	obviously	trente et un	31
mais	but	trente-deux, etc.	32, etc.
même si	even if	quarante	40
ou	or	cinquante	50
par contre	on the other hand	soixante	60

par exemple — for example

Had a look ☐ **Nearly there** ☐ **Nailed it** ☐

pendant que	while		
pourtant	however	soixante-dix	70
puis	then	soixante et onze	71
puisque	seeing that, since	soixante-douze	72
quand	when	soixante-treize	73
sans doute	undoubtedly, without doubt, probably	soixante-quatorze	74
		soixante-quinze	75
si	if	soixante-seize	76
y compris	including	soixante-dix-sept	77

Had a look ☐ **Nearly there** ☐ **Nailed it** ☐

soixante-dix-huit	78
soixante-dix-neuf	79

Numbers

Had a look ☐ **Nearly there** ☐ **Nailed it** ☐

un(e)	1		
deux	2		
trois	3	quatre-vingts	80
quatre	4	quatre-vingt-un	81
cinq	5	quatre-vingt-deux, etc.	82, etc.
six	6	quatre-vingt-dix	90
sept	7	quatre-vingt-onze	91
huit	8	quatre-vingt-douze, etc.	92, etc.

Had a look ☐ **Nearly there** ☐ **Nailed it** ☐

neuf	9		
dix	10		
onze	11	cent (m)	100
douze	12	cent un(e)	101
treize	13	cent vingt	120
quatorze	14	deux cents	200
quinze	15	mille (m)	1000
seize	16	mille cent	1100
dix-sept	17	deux mille	2000
dix-huit	18	un million (m)	1,000,000
dix-neuf	19	deux millions (m)	2,000,000
		premier/-ière	first
		deuxième	second
		onzième	eleventh
		vingt-et-unième	twenty-first

Had a look ☐ **Nearly there** ☐ **Nailed it** ☐

Had a look ☐ **Nearly there** ☐ **Nailed it** ☐

vingt	20
vingt et un	21
vingt-deux	22
vingt-trois	23

Opinions

vingt-quatre	24
vingt-cinq	25	à mon avis	in my opinion
vingt-six	26	absolument	absolutely
vingt-sept	27	bien entendu	of course
vingt-huit	28	bien sûr	of course
vingt-neuf	29	ça dépend	that depends

9

High-frequency words

ça m'énerve	it gets on my nerves	comme	as, like
ça me fait rire	it makes me laugh	la façon	way (manner)
ça me plaît	I like it	la fois	time (occasion)
ça m'est égal	it's all the same to me	le genre	type (kind of)
ça ne me dit rien	it means nothing to me, I don't fancy that, I don't feel like it	madame	Mrs, Madam
		mademoiselle	Miss
		monsieur	Mr, Sir
ça suffit	that's enough	le nombre	number
ça ne fait rien	it doesn't matter	le numéro	number (phone number)
ce n'est pas la peine	it's not worth it	par exemple	for example
d'accord	OK (in agreement)	quelqu'un	someone
j'en ai assez/marre	I've had enough	quelque chose	something
personnellement	personally	sauf	except
		la sorte	type (kind of)
		tout le monde	everybody

Had a look ☐   Nearly there ☐   Nailed it ☐

Had a look ☐   Nearly there ☐   Nailed it ☐

Other useful expressions

à bientôt	see you soon
à demain/vendredi	see you tomorrow/on Friday
bonne chance	good luck
bon courage	good luck
Ça s'écrit comment?	How do you spell that?
ça va	I'm fine, it's OK
comme çi, comme ça	so-so
désolé(e)	sorry
défense de	you are not allowed to
dommage	what a shame
excuse-/excusez-moi	(I'm) sorry (informal/formal)
il est interdit de	you are not allowed to

Time, frequency and sequencing expressions

à … heure(s)	at … o'clock
à … heure(s) et quart	at quarter past …
à … heure(s) et demie	at half past …
à … heure(s) moins le quart	at quarter to …
à la fois	at the same time
à l'avenir	in future, from now on
à l'heure	on time
à temps partiel	part-time
l'an (m)	year
l'année (f)	year
après	after
après-demain	the day after tomorrow
après-midi	afternoon
aujourd'hui	today
auparavant	formerly, in the past
avant	before
avant-hier	the day before yesterday
bientôt	soon

Had a look ☐   Nearly there ☐   Nailed it ☐

il faut	you must/one must
il y a	there is/are
je ne comprends pas	I don't understand
je ne sais pas	I don't know
merci (bien)	thank you (very much)
Qu'est-ce que cela veut dire?	What does that mean?
avec plaisir	with pleasure
tant mieux	all/so much the better
tant pis	too bad
voici	here is/are
voilà	there is/are (i.e. over there)
volontiers	with pleasure

Had a look ☐   Nearly there ☐   Nailed it ☐

d'abord	at first, firstly
dans le futur	in the future
d'habitude	usually
de bonne heure	early
le début	start
demain	tomorrow
dernier/-ière	last
de temps en temps	from time to time
déjà	already
de nouveau	again
en attendant	whilst waiting (for), meanwhile

Had a look ☐   Nearly there ☐   Nailed it ☐

Other useful little words

ça/cela	that
le chiffre	figure (number)
la chose	thing

High-frequency words

en avance	in advance
en ce moment	at the moment
en retard	late
en train de (faire…)	(to be) doing
en même temps	at the same time
encore une fois	once more, again
enfin	at last, finally
environ	about, approximately

Had a look ☐ **Nearly there** ☐ **Nailed it** ☐

la fin	end
hier	yesterday
il y a	ago
le jour	day
la journée	day
le lendemain	the next day
longtemps	for a long time
maintenant	now
le matin	morning
le mois	month
normalement	normally
la nuit	night
parfois	sometimes
le passé	past
pendant	during
plus tard	later
presque	almost, nearly
prochain	next

Had a look ☐ **Nearly there** ☐ **Nailed it** ☐

quelquefois	sometimes
rarement	rarely
récemment	recently
la semaine	week
seulement	only
le siècle	century
le soir	evening
soudain	suddenly
souvent	often
suivant	following
sur le point de (être)	(to be) about to
tard	late
tôt	early
toujours	always, still
tous les jours	every day
tout à coup	suddenly, all of a sudden
tout de suite	immediately
vite	quickly

Had a look ☐ **Nearly there** ☐ **Nailed it** ☐

Question words

Comment?	How?
Combien (de)?	How much, How many?
Que?	What?
Qu'est-ce qui?	What? (as subject)
Qu'est-ce que?	What? (as object)
Quoi?	What?
De quelle couleur?	What colour?
Comment?	What like?
À quelle heure?	(At) what time?
Quel/Quelle?	What/Which?
Quand?	When?
Où?	Where?
Lequel/Laquelle/ Lesquels/Lesquelles?	Which one(s)?
Qui?	Who?
Pourquoi?	Why?

Had a look ☐ **Nearly there** ☐ **Nailed it** ☐

Colours

blanc(he)	white
bleu(e)	blue
brun(e)	brown
châtain (invariable)	chestnut brown
clair(e)	light
foncé(e)	dark
gris(e)	grey
jaune	yellow
marron (invariable)	brown, chestnut brown
noir(e)	black
rose	pink
rouge	red
vert(e)	green
violet(te)	violet

Had a look ☐ **Nearly there** ☐ **Nailed it** ☐

Days, months and seasons of the year

lundi	Monday
mardi	Tuesday
mercredi	Wednesday
jeudi	Thursday
vendredi	Friday
samedi	Saturday
dimanche	Sunday

Had a look ☐ **Nearly there** ☐ **Nailed it** ☐

le mois	month
janvier	January
février	February

High-frequency words

mars	March	une boîte (de)	a tin (of), a box (of)
avril	April	une bouteille (de)	a bottle (of)
mai	May	une centaine (de)	about a hundred
juin	June	une douzaine (de)	a dozen
juillet	July	une tranche (de)	a slice (of)
août	August	une vingtaine (de)	about twenty
septembre	September		
octobre	October		
novembre	November		
décembre	December		

Had a look ☐ **Nearly there** ☐ **Nailed it** ☐

la saison	season
(au) printemps (m)	(in) spring
(en) été (m)	(in) summer
(en) automne (m)	(in) autumn
(en) hiver (m)	(in) winter

Had a look ☐ **Nearly there** ☐ **Nailed it** ☐

Countries

l'Algérie (f)	Algeria
l'Allemagne (f)	Germany
l'Angleterre (f)	England
l'Autriche (f)	Austria
la Belgique	Belgium
le Canada	Canada
la Chine	China
le Danemark	Denmark
la France	France
la Grande-Bretagne	Great Britain
la Grèce	Greece
la Hollande	Holland

Had a look ☐ **Nearly there** ☐ **Nailed it** ☐

Quantities and measures

assez (de)	enough
beaucoup (de)	a lot (of), many
un centilitre	centilitre
un centimètre	centimetre
demi	half
une gramme	gramme
un kilomètre	kilometre
un mètre	metre
moins (de)	less
encore (de)	(some) more
pas mal (de)	quite a few
(un) peu (de)	a little of, few
plus (de)	more
plusieurs	several
le poids	weight
la quantité	quantity
un quart	quarter
quelques	some
un tiers	third
trop (de)	too much, too many

l'Inde (f)	India
l'Irlande (f)	Ireland
l'Italie (f)	Italy
les Pays-Bas (m)	Netherlands
le Pakistan	Pakistan
la Russie	Russia
l'Écosse (f)	Scotland
le Sénégal	Senegal
l'Espagne (f)	Spain
la Suisse	Switzerland
la Tunisie	Tunisia
la Turquie	Turkey
le Royaume-Uni	United Kingdom
les États-Unis (m)	United States
le pays de Galles	Wales

Had a look ☐ **Nearly there** ☐ **Nailed it** ☐

Had a look ☐ **Nearly there** ☐ **Nailed it** ☐

Continents

l'Afrique (f)	Africa
l'Asie (f)	Asia
l'Australie (f)	Australia
l'Europe (f)	Europe
l'Amérique du Nord (f)	North America
l'Amérique du Sud (f)	South America

Had a look ☐ **Nearly there** ☐ **Nailed it** ☐

un kilo (de)	a kilo (of)
un litre (de)	a litre (of)
un morceau (de)	a piece (of)
un paquet (de)	a packet (of)
un peu (de)	a little (of)
un pot (de)	a jar (of)

High-frequency words

Nationalities
algérien(ne)	Algerian
allemand(e)	German
américain(e)	American
anglais(e)	English
autrichien(ne)	Austrian
belge	Belgian
britannique	British
canadien(ne)	Canadian
chinois(e)	Chinese
corse	Corsican
danois(e)	Danish
écossais(e)	Scottish
espagnol(e)	Spanish
européen(ne)	European
français(e)	French
gallois(e)	Welsh
grec(que)	Greek
hollandais(e)	Dutch

Had a look ☐ **Nearly there** ☐ **Nailed it** ☐

indien(ne)	Indian
irlandais(e)	Irish
italien(ne)	Italian
pakistanais(e)	Pakistani
russe	Russian
suisse	Swiss
tunisien(ne)	Tunisian
turque	Turkish

Had a look ☐ **Nearly there** ☐ **Nailed it** ☐

Geographical surroundings
à droite	on/to the right
à gauche	on/to the left
chez	at the house of
de chaque côté	from each side
de l'autre côté	from the other side
en bas	down(stairs)
en haut	up(stairs)
ici	here
là	there
là-bas	over there
la banlieue	suburb
la campagne	countryside
le centre-ville	town centre
la ville	town

Had a look ☐ **Nearly there** ☐ **Nailed it** ☐

loin de	far from
nulle part	nowhere
par	by
partout	everywhere
quelque part	somewhere
situé(e)	situated
tout droit	straight ahead
tout près	very near
toutes directions	all directions
l'est (m)	east
l'ouest (m)	west
le nord	north
le sud	south

Had a look ☐ **Nearly there** ☐ **Nailed it** ☐

Materials
l'argent (m)	silver
le béton	concrete
le bois	wood
le cuir	leather
le fer	iron
la laine	wool
l'or (m)	gold
la soie	silk
le verre	glass

Had a look ☐ **Nearly there** ☐ **Nailed it** ☐

Climate
l'averse (f)	shower
briller	to shine
le brouillard	fog
la brume	mist
la chaleur	heat
le ciel	sky
le climat	climate
couvert	overcast
doux	mild
l'éclair (m)	lightning
l'éclaircie (f)	bright spell
ensoleillé	sunny
faire beau	to be fine (weather)
faire mauvais	to be bad (weather)
geler	to freeze
la glace	ice
humide	humid, wet
la météo	weather forecast
mouillé	wet

Had a look ☐ **Nearly there** ☐ **Nailed it** ☐

High-frequency words

neiger	*to snow*
le nuage	*cloud*
nuageux	*cloudy*
l'ombre (f)	*shade, shadow*
l'orage (m)	*storm*
orageux	*stormy*
pleuvoir	*to rain*
la pluie	*rain*
sec	*dry*
la tempête	*storm*
le temps	*weather*
le tonnerre	*thunder*
tremper	*to soak*
le vent	*wind*

Had a look ☐ **Nearly there** ☐ **Nailed it** ☐

Social conventions

à plus tard	*see you later*
à tout à l'heure	*see you later*
allô	*hello (on the telephone)*
amitiés	*best wishes*
amuse-toi/amusez-vous bien!	*enjoy yourself/yourselves!*
au revoir	*goodbye*
au secours!	*help!*
bien sûr	*of course*
bon voyage	*have a good journey*
bonjour	*hello, good morning*
bonne journée	*have a good day*
bonne nuit	*goodnight*
bonne soirée	*have a good evening*
bonsoir	*good evening*
de rien	*don't mention it*
Je t'/vous en prie	*It's a pleasure*
non merci	*no thank you*
pardon?	*I beg your pardon?, Pardon?*
prière de	*please (request – formal)*
le rendez-vous	*meeting, meeting place*
rendez-vous à six heures	*meet you at 6 o'clock*
s'il te plaît/s'il vous plaît	*please (informal)/please (polite)*
salut	*hi*
veuillez	*please (request – formal)*

Had a look ☐ **Nearly there** ☐ **Nailed it** ☐

Words I should know for speaking and writing activities

La famille — *Family members*
le beau-père — *stepfather/father-in-law*
la belle-mère — *stepmother/mother-in-law*
le beau-frère — *brother-in-law*
la belle-sœur — *sister-in-law*
le demi-frère — *half-brother/stepbrother*
la demi-sœur — *half-sister/stepsister*
la fille — *daughter*
le fils — *son*
l'enfant — *child*
le petit-enfant — *grandchild*
le mari — *husband*
l'ex mari (m) — *ex-husband*
la femme — *wife*
l'ex femme (f) — *ex-wife*

Had a look ☐ **Nearly there** ☐ **Nailed it** ☐

Les adjectifs de personnalité — *Personality adjectives*
Il/Elle est … — *He/She is …*
agaçant(e) — *annoying*
aimable — *likeable*
amusant(e) — *amusing, funny*
arrogant(e) — *arrogant*
bavard(e) — *talkative, chatty*
charmant(e) — *charming*
drôle — *funny*
égoïste — *selfish*
fidèle — *loyal*
fort(e) — *strong*

Had a look ☐ **Nearly there** ☐ **Nailed it** ☐

généreux/-euse — *generous*
gentil(le) — *kind*
impatient(e) — *impatient*
jaloux/-ouse — *jealous*
méchant(e) — *nasty*
paresseux/-euse — *lazy*
poli(e) — *polite*
sage — *well-behaved, wise*
sensible — *sensitive*
sérieux/-euse — *serious*
sympa (invariable) — *nice*
têtu(e) — *stubborn, pig-headed*
travailleur/-euse — *hard-working*
triste — *sad*

Had a look ☐ **Nearly there** ☐ **Nailed it** ☐

Ma description physique — *My physical description*
J'ai les cheveux … — *I have … hair*
courts/longs/mi-longs — *short/long/mid-length*
raides/bouclés/frisés — *straight/curly*
noirs/bruns/châtain — *black/brown/chestnut*
blonds/roux/gris/blancs — *blond/red/grey/white*
J'ai les yeux … — *I have … eyes*
bleus/verts — *blue/green*
gris/marron — *grey/brown*
J'ai … — *I have …*
des boutons — *spots*
une barbe — *a beard*
une moustache — *a moustache*
Je suis … — *I am …*
petit(e)/grand(e) — *short/tall*
de taille moyenne — *of average height*
mince/gros(se) — *slim/fat*
beau/belle — *beautiful*
joli(e) — *pretty*
moche — *ugly*
Je porte des lunettes — *I wear glasses*

Had a look ☐ **Nearly there** ☐ **Nailed it** ☐

En ville — *In town*
la boîte de nuit — *nightclub*
le bowling — *bowling alley*
le café — *café*
le centre commercial — *shopping centre*
le cinéma — *cinema*
les magasins (m) — *shops*
la patinoire — *ice rink*
la piscine — *swimming pool*
la plage — *beach*
le théâtre — *theatre*
dans — *in*
derrière — *behind*
devant — *in front of*
entre — *between*
en face de — *opposite*
à côté de — *next to*
près de — *near*

Had a look ☐ **Nearly there** ☐ **Nailed it** ☐

Quand? — *When?*
aujourd'hui — *today*
demain — *tomorrow*
après-demain — *the day after tomorrow*

Module 1 Vocabulaire

ce matin	this morning	a les yeux qui inspirent confiance	has eyes which inspire (sb's) confidence
cet après-midi	this afternoon	On a les mêmes centres d'intérêt.	We have the same interests.
ce soir	tonight		

Had a look ☐ Nearly there ☐ Nailed it ☐

Had a look ☐ Nearly there ☐ Nailed it ☐

L'amitié / Friendship

Un(e) bon(ne) ami(e) est …	A good friend is …
de bonne humeur	in a good mood
compréhensif/-ive	understanding
équilibré(e)	balanced, level-headed
honnête	honest
indépendant(e)	independent
modeste	modest
patient(e)	patient
sûr(e) de lui/elle	self-confident
Un(e) bon(ne) ami(e) n'est pas …	A good friend is not …
de mauvaise humeur	in a bad mood
déprimé(e)	depressed
pessimiste	pessimistic
prétentieux/-euse	pretentious
vaniteux/-euse	conceited
Il/Elle …	He/She …
croit en moi	believes in me
dit toujours la vérité	always tells the truth
me fait rire	makes me laugh
prend soin de moi	takes care of me
voit le bon côté des choses	sees the positive side of things

Had a look ☐ Nearly there ☐ Nailed it ☐

Les traits de personnalité / Qualities

le sens de l'humour	a sense of humour
la patience	patience
la générosité	generosity
la gentillesse	kindness
la fidélité	loyalty
la modestie	modesty
l'honnêteté (f)	honesty
l'optimisme (m)	optimism

Had a look ☐ Nearly there ☐ Nailed it ☐

On décrit un(e) ami(e) / Describing a friend

Il/Elle …	He/She …
mesure 1,68 mètre	is 1m 68cm tall
semble timide	seems shy
porte un appareil dentaire	has a brace
a l'air cool	looks cool

Les rapports de famille / Family relationships

se confier à	to confide in
se disputer avec	to argue with
s'entendre bien avec	to get on well with
se fâcher contre	to get angry with
s'intéresser à	to be interested in
s'occuper de	to look after
s'aimer	to love each other
se chamailler	to bicker with each other
mort(e)/décédé(e)	dead
divorcé(e)(s)	divorced
séparé(e)(s)	separated

Had a look ☐ Nearly there ☐ Nailed it ☐

On décrit sa famille / Describing family members

adorable	adorable
débrouillard(e)	resourceful
dynamique	lively
énergique/plein(e) d'énergie	energetic
extraverti(e)	outgoing
fragile	fragile
instable	unstable
introverti(e)	introverted

Had a look ☐ Nearly there ☐ Nailed it ☐

On va sortir / Going out

Je vais/Tu vas/On va…	I'm going/You're going/We're going…
aller au match	to go to the match
faire les magasins	to go shopping
faire du patin à glace/du patinage	to go ice-skating
manger au fast-food	to eat in a fast-food restaurant
aller au cinéma	to go to the cinema
faire du skate	to go skateboarding
voir un spectacle	to see a show
jouer à des jeux vidéo	to play video games
venir chez moi	to come to my house
Tu veux venir?	Do you want to come?
Tu peux venir?	Can you come?
On se retrouve quand?	When will we meet?
… où?	Where …?

Module 1 Vocabulaire

… à quelle heure?	At what time …?
Tu y vas avec qui?	Who are you going there with?
… comment?	How …?
D'accord.	OK.
À plus!/À plus tard!	See you later!

Had a look ☐ **Nearly there** ☐ **Nailed it** ☐

On décrit une sortie — Describing a night out

hier soir	last night
à 20 heures	at 8 p.m.
d'abord	first of all
après	afterwards
puis/ensuite	then
J'ai …/Il/Elle a …/Nous avons …	I …/He/She …/We …
visité le musée	visited the museum
vu un match/une exposition	saw a match/an exhibition
mangé dans un restaurant	ate in a restaurant
refusé de manger	refused to eat
bu un coca	drank a cola
dit «au revoir»	said 'good-bye'
embrassé	kissed

Had a look ☐ **Nearly there** ☐ **Nailed it** ☐

Je suis …/Il/Elle est …/Nous sommes …	I …/He/She …/We …
allé(e)(s) à un pub	went to a pub
resté(e)(s) dehors sur la terrasse	stayed outside on the terrace
entré(e)(s) dans un restaurant	went into a restaurant
sorti(e)(s)	went out
parti(e)(s)	left
monté(e)(s) dans le bus	got on the bus
rentré(e)(s) à la maison	went home
tombé(e)(s) amoureux/-euse(s)	fell in love

Had a look ☐ **Nearly there** ☐ **Nailed it** ☐

Parler de son enfance — Talking about your childhood

Quand j'étais plus jeune, …	When I was younger, …
j'habitais avec (mon papa et ma maman)	I lived with (my mum and dad)
j'allais à l'école primaire	I went to primary school
j'avais (les cheveux blonds)	I had (blond hair)
j'étais (mignon(ne))	I was (cute)
je jouais (à «cache-cache»)	I played ('hide and seek')
j'aimais (les bonbons)	I liked (sweets)
je détestais (les épinards)	I hated (spinach)
je portais (un maillot du PSG)	I wore (a PSG shirt)
je rêvais d'être …	my dream was to be a …

Had a look ☐ **Nearly there** ☐ **Nailed it** ☐

Qui est-ce que tu admires? — Who do you admire?

Mon modèle s'appelle …	My role model is called …
Moi, j'admire …	Personally I admire …
Mon héros/Mon héroïne, c'est …	My hero/heroine is …
J'aimerais bien être comme lui/elle.	I would like to be like him/her.
J'admire sa créativité.	I admire his/her creativity.
Il/Elle …	He/She …
m'impressionne énormément	impresses me a lot
a travaillé très dur pour devenir …	worked very hard to become …
est devenu(e) …	became …
aide/a aidé …	helps/helped …
a/avait du courage/de la détermination	has/had courage/determination
est/était courageux/-euse face à des dangers terribles	is/was brave when faced with terrible danger
lutte/a lutté pour …	fights/fought for …
a obtenu …	obtained/got …
a sauvé la vie de …	saved the life of …
C'est un enfant adopté, comme moi.	He/She is adopted, like me.

Had a look ☐ **Nearly there** ☐ **Nailed it** ☐

17

Extra words I should know for reading and listening activities

Les descriptions	*Descriptions*	**Les verbes**	*Verbs*
laid(e)*	*ugly*	admirer	*to admire*
têtu(e)	*stubborn*	prendre soin de	*to take care of*
instable	*unstable*	se chamailler	*to argue*
débrouillard(e)	*resourceful*	porter	*to wear*
extraverti(e)	*extrovert*	dire la vérité	*to tell the truth*
introverti(e)	*introvert*	croire en quelqu'un	*to believe in someone*
agaçant(e)	*annoying*	briser en morceaux	*to break into pieces*
fidèle	*loyal*	diffuser	*to broadcast*
honnête	*honest*	envoyer	*to send*
sage	*wise*	libérer	*to free*
curieux/-euse	*curious*	voir le bon côté	*to see the good side*
déprimant(e)	*depressing*	rêver de	*to dream of*
défavorisé(e)	*underprivileged*	se fâcher contre	*to be angry with*
émouvant(e)	*touching*	captiver	*to captivate*
fascinant(e)	*fascinating*	tomber amoureux/ -euse de**	*to fall in love with*
turbulent(e)	*boisterous*	se confier à quelqu'un**	*to confide in someone*

Had a look ☐ **Nearly there** ☐ **Nailed it** ☐

Les expressions idiomatiques	*Idioms*
maigre comme un clou	*as thin as a rake*
le top du top!	*the best!*

refuser de faire quelque chose** — *to refuse to do something*
trouver quelque chose ... — *to find/think something is ...*

Had a look ☐ **Nearly there** ☐ **Nailed it** ☐

Had a look ☐ **Nearly there** ☐ **Nailed it** ☐

Les noms	*Nouns*
le héros	*hero*
l'héroïne (f)	*heroine*
le modèle	*model, example*
la légende	*legend, caption*
les traits	*characteristics*
des reflets roux	*red highlights*
des sabots	*clogs*
la couture	*sewing*
le foulard	*(head)scarf*
à un très jeune âge	*at a very young age*

Had a look ☐ **Nearly there** ☐ **Nailed it** ☐

---

*Many adjectives are cognates, i.e. words that are the same or similar in two languages but beware of false friends too!

The masculine adjective *laid* means 'ugly' and the last letter *d* is silent so watch out for the pronunciation.

**Remember that verbs in French don't always have the same prepositions after them that verbs in English do, for example:

to fall in love with *tomber amoureux de* ... (to fall in love of ...)

Module 2 Vocabulaire

Words I should know for speaking and writing activities

Le sport	Sport
Je fais …	I do/go …
du canoë-kayak	canoeing, kayaking
du footing	jogging
du hockey sur glace	ice hockey
du patinage	skating
du roller	roller skating
du vélo/cyclisme	cycling
de la boxe	boxing
de la danse	dancing
de la musculation	weightlifting
de la natation	swimming
de la planche à voile	windsurfing
de la voile	sailing
de l'escalade	climbing
de l'équitation	horse-riding
des randonnées	for walks
Je trouve ça …	I think it's …
bien/cool	good/cool
génial/super	great/super
passionnant	exciting
barbant/ennuyeux	boring
nul/stupide	rubbish/stupid

Had a look ☐   Nearly there ☐   Nailed it ☐

La musique	Music
Je joue …	I play …
du piano	the piano
du saxophone	the saxophone
du violon	the violin
de la batterie	drums
de la clarinette	the clarinet
de la flûte	the flute
de la guitare	the guitar
de la trompette	the trumpet
de l'accordéon	the accordion
Mon chanteur préféré, c'est …	My favourite singer is …
car j'aime ses paroles/ses mélodies	because I like his/her lyrics/tunes
J'aime aussi la musique de …	I also like …'s music.
Ça me donne envie de …	It makes me want to …
Ça me rend …	It makes me …
J'ai téléchargé/acheté …	I downloaded/bought …
Je n'aime pas du tout la musique de …	I don't like …'s music at all.
Je déteste …	I hate …

Had a look ☐   Nearly there ☐   Nailed it ☐

La technologie	Technology
Je fais …	I do …
beaucoup de choses	lots of things
des quiz/des recherches pour mes devoirs	quizzes/research for my homework
Je fais des achats.	I buy things/make purchases.
Je vais sur mes sites préférés/des blogs/des forums.	I go on my favourite sites/blogs/forums.
J'envoie des e-mails/mails.	I send emails.
Je joue à des jeux en ligne.	I play games online.

Had a look ☐   Nearly there ☐   Nailed it ☐

Films et télé	Films and TV
J'aime/J'adore les …	I like/love …
Je (ne) suis (pas) fan de …	I am (not) a fan of …
Je n'aime pas …	I don't like …
J'ai une passion pour les …	I am passionate about …
J'ai horreur des …	I hate/can't stand …
films de gangsters/d'action	gangster/action films
films d'aventure/d'horreur	adventure/horror films
films d'arts martiaux	martial arts films
films de science-fiction	science fiction films
Je préfère …	I prefer …
les documentaires	documentaries
les jeux télévisés	game shows
les magazines	magazine programmes
les séries	series
les actualités	current affairs programmes
les émissions de musique/de sport/jeunesse/de télé-réalité	music/sports/youth/reality TV programmes
Mon émission préférée, c'est …	My favourite programme is …
Je trouve ça …	I find it …
Je pense que c'est …	I think that it's …

Had a look ☐   Nearly there ☐   Nailed it ☐

Parler de sport	Talking about sport
Je fais de l'escrime/du footing depuis (quatre ans).	I've been doing fencing/jogging for (four years).

19

Module 2 Vocabulaire

Français	English
Je pratique le trampoline depuis (trois mois).	I've been trampolining for (three months).
On joue au basket ensemble depuis (trois ans).	We've been playing basketball together for (three years).
J'aime beaucoup ça car c'est …	I like it a lot because it's …
élégant/facile	elegant/easy
ludique/sympa	fun/nice
rapide/beau	fast/pleasant
C'est un sport qui est bon pour …	It's a sport that is good for …
le corps/le cœur	the body/the heart
le mental/la concentration	the mind/concentration
… et qui demande …	… and which requires …
une excellente forme physique	excellent physical condition
une bonne coordination	good coordination
de l'endurance	endurance
de bons réflexes	good reflexes
Ça m'aide à décompresser.	It helps me to relax.
Ça me fait du bien.	It does me good.
Je préfère les sports individuels.	I prefer individual sports.
Je respire.	I breathe.
Je me fixe des objectifs.	I set goals for myself.
J'oublie mes soucis.	I forget my worries.

Had a look ☐ **Nearly there** ☐ **Nailed it** ☐

Ma vie d'internaute / My life online

Français	English
Je suis passionné(e) de …	I am passionate about/a huge fan of …
photographie/cinéma/musique	photography/cinema/music
Il y a (deux mois), j'ai créé …	(Two months) ago, I created …
une page Facebook	a Facebook page
une chaîne YouTube	a YouTube channel
une station de radio	a radio station
un blog	a blog
Ça (ne) marche (pas) très bien.	It's (not) working very well.
J'ai beaucoup d'abonnés et de mentions «J'aime».	I have lots of subscribers and likes.
Je vais travailler avec mon ami/ma sœur/prof …	I'm going to work with my friend/sister/teacher …
car il/elle est plus/moins … que moi	because he/she is more/less … than me
arrogant(e)/créatif/-ve	arrogant/creative
modeste/patient(e)	modest/patient
optimiste/organisé(e)	optimistic/organised
sérieux/-euse/technophobe	serious/technophobic
Nous allons créer …	We're going to create …

Had a look ☐ **Nearly there** ☐ **Nailed it** ☐

La lecture / Books and reading

Français	English
Quand j'avais X ans, je lisais …	When I was X years old, I read …
J'aimais …	I liked …
Avant, avec mes enfants, on lisait …	In the past, I read … with my children.
des histoires/des romans	stories/novels
des livres illustrés/classiques	illustrated books/classics
des livres pour enfants/des journaux	children's books/newspapers
Maintenant, je lis …	Now I read …
sur ma tablette/mon ordi	on my tablet/my computer

Had a look ☐ **Nearly there** ☐ **Nailed it** ☐

Sur Internet / On the internet

Français	English
Maintenant/Aujourd'hui, les jeunes …	Now/Today, young people …
lisent des blogs/des textos/des tweets	read blogs/texts/tweets
passent tout leur temps sur leur portable	spend all their time on their mobile
Je trouve ça génial.	I find that great.
Je trouve que c'est bien/mieux/un peu dommage.	I find that it's good/better/a bit of a shame.
À mon avis, Internet a tué les joies de la lecture.	In my opinion, the internet has killed the joy of reading.

Had a look ☐ **Nearly there** ☐ **Nailed it** ☐

Mes émissions préférées / My favourite TV programmes

Français	English
Mon émission de télé préférée, c'est …	My favourite TV programme is …
C'est (un docu-réalité) qui parle de …	It's (a reality documentary) about …
Je le/la regarde …	I watch it …
toutes les semaines	every week
tous les jours/mois	every day/month
Je le/la trouve formidable/super/génial(e).	I find it amazing/fantastic/great.
Je ne le rate/manque jamais.	I never miss it.

Module 2 Vocabulaire

Je ne le/la regarde jamais.	I never watch it.
Je le/la trouve débile/vulgaire.	I find it idiotic/crude.
J'adore les animateurs/animatrices.	I love the presenters.
Les acteurs sont excellents/ne sont pas crédibles.	The actors are excellent/not believable.
Le scénario n'a aucun rapport avec la réalité.	The script bears no relation to reality.
Je le/la regarde en version originale.	I watch it in the original language.
Avant, je regardais/nous regardions ...	Before, I/we used to watch ...
Maintenant, j'ai tendance à regarder ...	Now, I tend to watch ...
en direct sur la TNT	live on terrestrial TV
en replay/streaming	recorded/streamed

Had a look ☐ **Nearly there** ☐ **Nailed it** ☐

X compte parmi les acteurs les plus connus et les plus appréciés au monde.	X is one of the best-known and best-regarded actors in the world.
J'adore ses films et je les recommande.	I love his/her films and I recommend them.
Je vais voir son prochain film très bientôt.	I'm going to see his/her next film very soon.

Had a look ☐ **Nearly there** ☐ **Nailed it** ☐

Le cinéma / Cinema

Je suis passionné(e) de cinéma.	I'm passionate/mad about cinema.
J'adore ...	I love ...
J'admire ...	I admire ...
Je suis fan de ... depuis	I'm a fan of ... since ...
Il est le plus ...	He is the most ...
Elle est la plus ...	She is the most ...
beau/belle	good-looking, beautiful
intelligent(e)	intelligent
talentueux/-euse	talented
élégant(e)	elegant
doué(e)	gifted, talented
célèbre	famous
chic	chic
Chez lui/elle, il y a très peu ...	With him/her, there is very little ...
de prétention	pretentiousness
de vanité	vanity
d'arrogance	arrogance

Had a look ☐ **Nearly there** ☐ **Nailed it** ☐

Il/Elle est extrêmement modeste/sincère/humble.	He/she is extremely modest/sincere/humble.
J'ai vu le film ... il y a un moment et depuis, je suis fan.	I saw the ... film some time ago and since then, I've been a fan.
Apparemment, quand il/elle était jeune ...	Apparently, when he/she was young ...

Extra words I should know for reading and listening activities

Les descriptions	*Descriptions*	**Les idées**	*Concepts*
impatient(e)	*impatient*	la généalogie	*genealogy*
charismatique	*charismatic*	la souplesse	*flexibility*
arrogant(e)	*arrogant*	le corps	*body*
modeste	*modest*	le mental	*mind*
créatif/-ve	*creative*	l'endurance (f)	*endurance, stamina*
ludique	*fun*	la persévérance	*perseverance*
motivant(e)	*motivating*	le projet	*plan*
fédérateur/-rice	*unifying*	les joies (f)	*joys*
urbain(e)	*urban*	la perte de temps	*waste of time*
collectif/-ve	*collective*		

Had a look ☐ Nearly there ☐ Nailed it ☐

Had a look ☐ Nearly there ☐ Nailed it ☐

Les nouvelles technologies	*New technologies*
les mentions (f)	*likes*
les abonné(e)s	*subscribers*
l'ambiance (f)	*atmosphere*
l'ordinateur/ordi (m)	*computer*
la chanson	*song*
le/la chanteur/-euse	*singer*
le portable	*mobile phone*
les blogs (m)*	*blogs*
les forums (m)*	*forums*
les réseaux sociaux (m)	*social networks*
les jeux en ligne (m)	*online games*
l'écran (m)	*screen*
la tablette*	*tablet*
la toile	*the web*
les textos (m)*	*texts*

Les expressions	*Expressions*
Ça m'énerve!**	*That annoys me!*
Ça m'amuse!**	*That makes me laugh!*
Ça marche bien!**	*That works well!*
Ça me passionne!**	*That fascinates me!*
Je décompresse!	*I chill out!*
Je suis passionné(e) de …	*I'm a keen …*
Je prends plaisir à …	*I enjoy …*

Had a look ☐ Nearly there ☐ Nailed it ☐

Had a look ☐ Nearly there ☐ Nailed it ☐

*Lots of new technology-related words are the same in French as in English, for example, *des blogs*.

**French people use *Ça* over and over in everyday language – try to learn as many expressions as you can with it in to increase your fluency!

Module 3 Vocabulaire

Words I should know for speaking and writing activities

Repas et nourriture	Meals and food
Je bois/mange/prends …	I drink/eat/have …
du café/lait/jus d'orange	coffee/milk/orange juice
du pain grillé/beurre	toast/butter
du yaourt/miel	yogurt/honey
du poulet/jambon/poisson	chicken/ham/fish
du saucisson/fromage	sausage/cheese
du pain/riz	bread/rice
du chou-fleur/raisin	cauliflower/grapes
de la confiture/glace	jam/ice cream
de la soupe/viande	soup/meat
de la mousse au chocolat/tarte au citron	chocolate mousse/lemon tart
de l'eau (minérale) (f)	(mineral) water
des fruits (m)/bananes (f)	fruit/bananas
des fraises (f)/pêches (f)	strawberries/peaches
des pommes (f)/poires (f)	apples/pears
des légumes (m)/petits pois (m)	vegetables/peas
des champignons (m)/haricots verts (m)	mushrooms/green beans
des carottes (f)/pommes de terre (f)	carrots/potatoes
des céréales (f)/pâtes (f)	cereal/pasta
des crudités (f)/œufs (m)	crudités/eggs

Had a look ☐ Nearly there ☐ Nailed it ☐

Je ne mange pas de viande.	I don't eat meat.
Je suis végétarien(ne).	I'm vegetarian.
un paquet de …	a packet of …
un kilo de …	a kilo of …
une bouteille de …	a bottle of …
un pot de …	a jar/pot of …
cinq cents grammes de …	500 grams of …
quatre tranches de …	four slices of …
un morceau de …	a piece of …
un litre de …	a litre of …
une boîte de …	a tin/can of …
Il faut aller …	You need to go …
à la boucherie	to the butcher's
à la boulangerie	to the baker's
à la charcuterie	to the deli/pork butcher's
à la pâtisserie	to the cake shop
à l'épicerie (f)	to the grocer's
au marché	to the market

Had a look ☐ Nearly there ☐ Nailed it ☐

Les vêtements	Clothes
D'habitude, je porte …	Usually I wear …
Je vais mettre …	I'm going to put on …
J'ai mis …	I put on …
un blouson	a jacket
un chapeau	a hat
un collant	tights
un costume	a suit
un jean moulant	skinny jeans
un manteau	a coat
un pantalon	trousers
un polo	a polo shirt
un pull	a sweater

Had a look ☐ Nearly there ☐ Nailed it ☐

un sac à main	a handbag
un short	shorts
un sweat à capuche	a hoody
un tee-shirt	a T-shirt
une casquette	a cap
une ceinture	a belt
une chemise	a shirt
une cravate	a tie
une écharpe	a scarf
une mini-jupe	a mini-skirt
une robe	a dress
une veste	a jacket
des baskets (f)	trainers
des bottes (f)	boots
des chaussettes (f)	socks
des chaussures (f)	shoes
des gants (m)	gloves
des lunettes de soleil (f)	sunglasses

Had a look ☐ Nearly there ☐ Nailed it ☐

blanc(he)(s)	white
bleu(e)(s)	blue
gris(e)(s)	grey
jaune(s)	yellow
kaki	khaki
marron	brown
mauve(s)	purple
noir(e)(s)	black
orange	orange
rose(s)	pink
rouge(s)	red

M 3

23

Module 3 Vocabulaire

vert(e)(s)	green
en coton/cuir/laine/soie	(made of) cotton/leather/wool/silk
rayé(e)	striped
à carreaux	checked
de marque	designer
habillé(e)	smart
de couleur vive	brightly-coloured
multicolore	multi-coloured
foncé(e)	dark

Had a look ☐ Nearly there ☐ Nailed it ☐

La vie quotidienne / *Daily life*

J'ai cours …	I have lessons …
tous les jours sauf …	every day except …
(cinq) jours par semaine	(five) days a week
Je vais au lycée …	I go to school …
en bus/en scooter/en voiture/à pied	by bus/by moped/by car/on foot
Les jours d'école, …	On school days …
je dois me lever tôt	I have to get up early
je prends mon petit-déjeuner	I have my breakfast
je quitte la maison	I leave the house
Le dimanche, …	On Sundays …
je peux rester au lit/faire la grasse matinée	I can stay in bed/have a lie-in
Le soir, …	In the evening …
je dois faire mes devoirs	I have to do my homework
je mange avec ma famille	I eat with my family
je regarde un peu la télé	I watch a bit of TV
Le mercredi/samedi après-midi, …	On Wednesday/Saturday afternoon …
je peux me détendre un peu	I can relax a bit
je reste à la maison/chez moi	I stay at home
Le week-end, …	At the weekend …
je sors avec mes copains	I go out with friends
je dois aider ma mère/mon père	I have to help my mum/dad
je vais au cinéma/au bowling	I go to the cinema/bowling

Had a look ☐ Nearly there ☐ Nailed it ☐

Les repas de fêtes / *Food for special occasions*

Ma fête préférée est …	My favourite festival is …
Noël/le 5 novembre/Hanoukka/Aïd el-Fitr/Diwali	Christmas/5 November/Hanukkah/Eid al-Fitr/Diwali
parce que j'adore …	because I love …
D'habitude, je le/la fête …	I usually celebrate it …
en famille/chez nous	with my family/at home
chez mon/ma/mes …/avec …	at my …'s house/with …
On fait/décore/se souhaite …	We do/decorate/wish each other …
D'abord, on mange/boit … suivi(e) par …	First we eat/drink …, followed by …
de la dinde	turkey
une bûche de Noël	Yule log
Dedans, il y a …	Inside, there is …
C'est mon/ma/mes … qui prépare(nt) …	My … prepare(s) …
Après le repas, on …	After the meal we …
s'offre (des cadeaux)	give each other (presents)
admire (le sapin de Noël)	admire the (Christmas tree)
chante/danse	sing/dance

Had a look ☐ Nearly there ☐ Nailed it ☐

Les repas à la maison / *Meals at home*

Du lundi au vendredi, je prends	From Monday to Friday I have
le petit-déjeuner à … heures.	breakfast at …
Le week-end, je prends mon petit-déjeuner plus tard.	At the weekend I have my breakfast later.
Je grignote après l'école.	I have a snack after school.
Je ne grignote jamais en dehors des repas.	I never snack between meals.
Je regarde la télé en mangeant le soir.	I watch TV while eating in the evening.
Dans ma famille, on ne regarde pas la télé en mangeant.	In our family, we don't watch TV while eating.
On dîne en famille tous les jours.	We have dinner as a family every day.

Had a look ☐ Nearly there ☐ Nailed it ☐

Félicitations! / *Congratulations!*

Je suis né(e) en …	I was born in …
Je viens de fêter …	I have just celebrated …
Il y a (trois) mois, j'ai fêté …	(Three) months ago I celebrated …
C'était mon quatorzième/quinzième anniversaire.	It was my fourteenth/fifteenth birthday.
J'ai reçu beaucoup de …	I received lots of …

Module 3 Vocabulaire

J'ai invité … à un barbecue/une fête chez moi.	I invited … to a barbecue/party at my house.
Je suis allé(e) au mariage (de mon cousin) à la mairie avec toute ma famille.	I went to (my cousin's) wedding at the town hall with all my family.
On a mangé/écouté/dansé/joué/fait/vu …	We ate/listened to/danced/played/did/saw …
C'était une excellente soirée!	It was an excellent evening!
Pour fêter mon prochain anniversaire, je vais …	To celebrate my next birthday, I'm going to …

Had a look ☐ **Nearly there** ☐ **Nailed it** ☐

Les fêtes en France — *Festivals in France*

le jour férié	public holiday
le jour de l'An	New Year's Day
la fête des Rois/l'Épiphanie (f)	Twelfth Night/Epiphany
la Chandeleur	Candlemas
la Saint-Valentin	St Valentine's Day
Mardi Gras	Shrove Tuesday
1er Avril	April Fool's Day
Pâques	Easter
la fête du Travail	May Day/Labour Day
la fête des Mères	Mother's Day
la fête de la Musique	music festival in France on 21 June
la fête nationale	Bastille Day, 14 July
la Nuit Blanche	first Saturday of October, when many museums and art galleries stay open all night
la Toussaint	All Saints' Day
le jour de Noël	Christmas Day
la Saint-Sylvestre	New Year's Eve

Had a look ☐ **Nearly there** ☐ **Nailed it** ☐

Module 3 Vocabulaire

Extra words I should know for reading and listening activities

La nourriture — *Food*
le chou-fleur	*cauliflower*
la bûche de Noël	*yule log*
le réveillon	*New Year's Eve meal*
la galette des rois	*special cake made to be eaten at Epiphany*
les verrines (f)	*verrines/tumblers/bite-size desserts*
la fève	*lucky charm put into the 'galette des rois'*
les épinards (m)	*spinach*
le saumon	*salmon*
la salade composée	*mixed salad*
le croquembouche	*profiterole-based dessert, built into a tower, quite often eaten as a cake at weddings*

Had a look ☐   Nearly there ☐   Nailed it ☐

Les jours de fête — *Celebrations*
la fête	*festivities, festival*
les noces d'argent (f)	*silver wedding anniversary*
la bague	*ring*
la mairie	*town hall*
le témoin	*witness*
le feu d'artifice	*fireworks*
le déguisement	*costume*
la reine	*queen*
les chars fleuris (m)	*flower-decked floats*
la Toussaint	*All Souls' Day (1 November)*
la Nuit Blanche	*an all-night or night-time arts festival, held every year in France on the first Saturday in October, where all museums, private and public art galleries and other cultural institutions are open free to the public*
le pays natal	*country of birth*

Had a look ☐   Nearly there ☐   Nailed it ☐

Décrire les fêtes — *Describing celebrations*
apprécié(e)	*appreciated*
partagé(e)	*shared*
attaché(e)	*attached*
élaboré(e)	*developed*
multicolore	*multicoloured*
prêt(e)	*ready*
loué(e)	*hired/rented*
gratuit(e)	*free*
alimentaire	*foodstuff*
pareil(le)	*same*
fier/-ière de	*proud of*
en soie*	*made of silk*
en laine*	*made of wool*
de marque*	*branded*
de couleur vive*	*brightly coloured*

Had a look ☐   Nearly there ☐   Nailed it ☐

Verbes — *Verbs*
se pacser	*to have a civil partnership*
grignoter	*to snack*
fêter	*to celebrate*
cacher	*to hide*
faire la grasse matinée	*to lie in*
être allergique à …	*to be allergic to …*
avoir horreur de …	*to hate …*
avoir lieu**	*to take place*
ajouter	*to add*
en mangeant …	*whilst eating …*

Had a look ☐   Nearly there ☐   Nailed it ☐

Les expressions idiomatiques — *Idioms*
Ne t'en fais pas!	*Don't worry about it!*
Et voilà!	*There you go!*

Had a look ☐   Nearly there ☐   Nailed it ☐

⭐ *Use *en* to refer to what something is made of.*
Elle porte une robe en soie et lui un costume en laine.
Use the preposition *de* to indicate what type of item it is and to convey more description.
Benjamin aime les vêtements de marque et de couleur vive.

⭐ **The verb *avoir* is used for many idiomatic expressions that will help you sound more fluent in your writing and your speaking.
Examples: *avoir lieu* to take place, *en avoir marre* to have had enough.
La fête a lieu le 23 septembre. The festival takes place on the 23rd of September.
Le travail, c'est dur! J'en ai marre! Working is hard! I've had enough!

Module 4 Vocabulaire

Words I should know for speaking and writing activities

Où j'habite	**Where I live**
J'habite …	I live …
Ma famille et moi habitons …	My family and I live …
On habite …	We live …
dans une ville historique/touristique	in an historic/touristy town
dans un petit village	in a small village
au bord de la mer	at the seaside
au centre-ville	in the town centre
à la campagne/montagne	in the countryside/mountains
en ville	in town
en Angleterre/Écosse/Irlande (du Nord)/Afrique	in England/Scotland/(Northern) Ireland/Africa
au Maroc/pays de Galles	in Morocco/Wales
aux Antilles	in the West Indies
à Paris/Birmingham	in Paris/Birmingham

Had a look ☐ Nearly there ☐ Nailed it ☐

dans le nord-est du/de la/de l'/des …	in the north-east of …
le nord/le nord-est	north/north-east
l'est/le sud-est	east/south-east
le sud/le sud-ouest	south/south-west
l'ouest/le nord-ouest	west/north-west
Dans ma région, il y a …	In my region there is/are …
des vignobles/stations de ski	vineyards/ski resorts
des collines/forêts	hills/forests
des fermes/champs	farms/fields
un port de pêche	a fishing port
un lac	a lake
C'est super parce qu'en hiver/en été, on peut (faire du ski/de l'escalade).	It's great because in winter/summer, you can (go skiing/climbing).

Had a look ☐ Nearly there ☐ Nailed it ☐

Le temps	**Weather**
Il fait beau/mauvais.	The weather's good/bad.
Il fait chaud/froid.	It's hot/cold.
Il y a du soleil.	It's sunny.
Il y a du brouillard/du vent.	It's foggy/windy.
Il y a un orage.	There's a storm.
Il pleut/neige/gèle.	It's raining/snowing/icy.
Ici, le climat est humide/sec.	Here, the climate is wet/dry.
Il peut faire très chaud/froid/doux.	It can be very hot/cold/mild.
Il ne fait pas trop chaud/froid …	It's not too hot/cold …

au printemps	in spring
en été/automne/hiver	in summer/autumn/winter

Had a look ☐ Nearly there ☐ Nailed it ☐

Les transports	**Transport**
Je vais/peux aller au collège …	I go/can go to school …
à pied/vélo	on foot/by bike
en train/métro/car/voiture/bus	by train/underground/coach/car/bus
Les transports en commun sont bons.	The public transport is good.

Had a look ☐ Nearly there ☐ Nailed it ☐

M 4

En ville	**In town**
Il y a …	There is/are …
un château	a castle
un centre de loisirs	a leisure centre
un marché	a market
un musée	a museum
un parc/jardin public	a (public) park
un stade	a stadium
un supermarché	a supermarket
un théâtre	a theatre
une bibliothèque	a library
une cathédrale	a cathedral
une église	a church
une gare (SNCF)	a (train) station
une mairie	a town hall
une mosquée	a mosque
une pharmacie	a chemist
une poste (un bureau de poste)	a post office
des hôtels	hotels

Had a look ☐ Nearly there ☐ Nailed it ☐

beaucoup de magasins	lots of shops
Il n'y a pas de …	There isn't a/aren't any …
Est-ce qu'il y a un/une/des … près d'ici/par ici?	Is/Are there a/some … near here?
Va/Allez tout droit.	Go straight on.
Tourne/Tournez à droite/gauche.	Turn right/left.
Prends/Prenez la première/deuxième droite/gauche.	Take the first/second road on the right/left.
Continue/Continuez jusqu'au carrefour/jusqu'aux feux	Continue as far as the crossroads/traffic lights
Traverse/Traversez la place/le pont.	Cross the square/bridge.
Descends/Descendez la rue.	Go down the road.

Module 4 Vocabulaire

C'est … | It's …
(assez) loin/tout près | (quite) a long way/very close
sur ta/votre droite/gauche | on your right/left
au coin | on the corner
en face (du/de la/de l'/des) | opposite
à côté (du/de la/de l'/des) | next to

Had a look ☐ Nearly there ☐ Nailed it ☐

Ma région / My region
Ma région/Une région que je connais bien, c'est … | My region/A region that I know well is …
C'est dans le (nord/sud) de … | It's in the (north/south) of …
près de la Manche/la frontière allemande/espagnole | near the English Channel/the German/Spanish border
J'y habite depuis …/J'y vais … | I have lived there since …/I have been going there …
Le paysage/La côte est vraiment magnifique/impressionnant(e). | The landscape/coast is really wonderful/impressive.
On peut y faire/visiter/voir … | You can do/visit/see … there.
La région est connue pour … | The region is known for …
Une personne célèbre qui est née en …, c'est … | A famous person who was born in … is …

Had a look ☐ Nearly there ☐ Nailed it ☐

Les renseignements / Information
Qu'est-ce qu'on va faire à …? | What are we going to do in …?
Je veux absolument (faire une promenade en bateau). | I definitely want to (go on a boat trip).
J'ai envie de (louer un bateau). | I feel like (hiring a boat).
Ça m'intéresse de voir … | I'm interested in seeing …
Je tiens à (visiter l'aquarium). | I'm keen on (visiting the aquarium).
Je voudrais aller au/à la/à l'/aux … | I would like to go to …
J'aimerais bien monter à la/au … | I would like to go up …
Je ne veux pas rater/manquer (l'exposition sur) … | I don't want to miss (the exhibition on) …
Bonne idée. Pourquoi pas? | Good idea. Why not?
Je veux bien faire ça aussi. | I want to do that too.
D'accord. Ça m'est égal. | OK. I don't mind.
Ça ne me dit rien. | I don't fancy that.
Je n'en ai pas tellement envie. | I don't really feel like it.
Ça a l'air nul! | That sounds rubbish!

Had a look ☐ Nearly there ☐ Nailed it ☐

Ville de rêve ou ville de cauchemar? / Dream town or nightmare town?
J'habite à … | I live in …
C'est un petit village/une grande ville dans … | It's a small village/big town in …
J'habite dans la banlieue/un quartier de … | I live in the suburbs/a district of …
Ce qui me plaît ici, c'est qu'il y a … | What I like is that …
En été/hiver, on peut … | In summer/winter, you can …
Le problème, c'est que/qu' … | The problem is that …
il n'y a pas assez de (magasins/ espaces verts) | there is/are not enough (shops/green spaces)
il n'y a plus de (cinéma) | there is/are no longer (a cinema)
il n'y a ni (parc) ni (aire de jeux) | there is neither (a park) nor (a play area)
il n'y a aucun (bowling) | there isn't a (single) (bowling alley)
il n'y a aucune (zone piétonne) | there isn't a (single) (pedestrian area)
il n'y a qu'un seul (magasin) | there is only one (shop)
il n'y a qu'une seule (rue) | there is just one (street)
il n'y a rien pour les jeunes | there is nothing for young people
il n'y a pas grand-chose à faire | there's not a lot to do

Had a look ☐ Nearly there ☐ Nailed it ☐

Il y a … | There is/are …
beaucoup de monde/de voitures | lots of people/cars
trop de circulation/de gens | too much traffic/too many people
tellement de bruit/de gens au chômage | so much noise/so many people out of work
peu de travail/de transports en commun/commerces | not much work/public transport/not many businesses
toujours des déchets par terre | always litter on the ground
plusieurs boîtes de nuit/cafés/restaurants | several nightclubs/cafés/restaurants
Le bowling a fermé. | The bowling alley has closed down.

Module 4 Vocabulaire

C'est sale/(trop) tranquille/très animé. *It's dirty/(too) quiet/very lively.*
Ce n'est jamais tranquille. *It's never quiet.*
Je trouve ça triste/déprimant/affreux/nul/désagréable. *I find that sad/depressing/awful/rubbish/unpleasant.*
En général, je (ne) suis (pas) content(e) de mon village/quartier/ma ville. *In general, I am (not) happy with my village/district/town.*

Had a look ☐ **Nearly there** ☐ **Nailed it** ☐

Les projets / Plans
Qu'est-ce qu'on fera? *What shall we do?*
On ira pique-niquer dans le parc. *We'll have a picnic in the park.*
Ce sera génial! *That will be great!*
Je resterai à la maison. *I will stay at home.*
Je regarderai un film. *I will watch a film.*
Je jouerai à des jeux vidéo/au football. *I will play video games/football.*
On ne fera pas de barbecue. *We won't have a barbecue.*
On mangera dans un restaurant. *We will eat in a restaurant.*

Had a look ☐ **Nearly there** ☐ **Nailed it** ☐

Quel temps fera-t-il? / What will the weather be like?
Il y aura … *There will be …*
du vent *wind*
du soleil *sun*
du tonnerre *thunder*
de la grêle *hail*
de la pluie *rain*
des averses *showers*
des éclairs *lightning*
des éclaircies *sunny intervals*
Il fera … *It will be …*
beau/chaud/froid/frais *fine/hot/cold/cool*
Le temps sera … brumeux/ensoleillé nuageux/orageux variable *The weather will be … misty/sunny cloudy/stormy changeable*
Le ciel sera bleu/gris/couvert. *The sky will be blue/grey/overcast.*
Les températures seront en baisse/en hausse. *The temperatures will be going down/going up.*

Had a look ☐ **Nearly there** ☐ **Nailed it** ☐

En pleine action! / Taking action
J'ai/Nous avons … *I/We have …*
collecté de l'argent *collected money*
vendu nos vieux jeux et jouets *sold our old games and toys*
lavé des voitures *washed cars*
acheté (de la peinture) *bought (paint)*
planté des arbres *planted trees*
lancé une pétition en ligne *launched an online petition*
obtenu presque 2 000 signatures *obtained nearly 2,000 signatures*
écrit un article dans le journal local *written an article in the local newspaper*

Had a look ☐ **Nearly there** ☐ **Nailed it** ☐

Le week-end prochain, nous irons là-bas pour … *Next weekend, we will go there to …*
ramasser les déchets *pick up litter*
nettoyer la salle *clean the room*
repeindre les murs *repaint the walls*
La semaine prochaine, on finira d'installer/de construire … *Next week, we will finish installing/building …*
un passage piéton *a pedestrian crossing*
un panneau *a sign*
une aire de jeux *a play area*

Had a look ☐ **Nearly there** ☐ **Nailed it** ☐

M 4

29

Module 4 Vocabulaire

Extra words I should know for reading and listening activities

La géographie	*Geography*
la principauté	principality
le paysage	landscape, scenery
les Bretons (m)*	people from Brittany
le panorama	panorama
le quartier	area
la province	province
le milieu	environment
les gorges (f)	gorges
les collines (f)	hills

Had a look ☐ **Nearly there** ☐ **Nailed it** ☐

Les sports extrêmes	*Extreme sports*
le canyoning	canyoning
le saut à l'élastique	bungee jumping

Had a look ☐ **Nearly there** ☐ **Nailed it** ☐

Le climat	*Climate*
le changement climatique	climate change
le climat	climate
le mistral	cold, northerly wind
la vague de chaleur	heatwave
la canicule	scorching heat, heatwave
la tempête	storm
l'ouragan (m)	hurricane
le cyclone	cyclone

Had a look ☐ **Nearly there** ☐ **Nailed it** ☐

En route!	*On the road!*
la limite de vitesse	speed limit
les transports en commun (m)	public transport
les déchets (m)	rubbish
la circulation	traffic
les routes (f)	roads
les distributeurs de billets (m)	cash machines
les morts (f)	deaths

Had a look ☐ **Nearly there** ☐ **Nailed it** ☐

En ville	*In town*
les missions de volontariat (f)	volunteering
les promenades commentées (f)	guided tours
les stations de ski (f)	ski resorts
les stations balnéaires (f)	seaside resorts

Had a look ☐ **Nearly there** ☐ **Nailed it** ☐

Les milieux	*Environments*
défavorisé (e)	underprivileged
déprimant (e)	depressing
majestueux/-euse	majestic
véritable	real
les parfumeries (f)	perfumeries
les vignobles (m)	vineyards
les ateliers (m) de poterie (f)	potteries

Had a look ☐ **Nearly there** ☐ **Nailed it** ☐

Les verbes	*Verbs*
arrêter	to stop
causer	to cause
ramasser	to collect
collecter	to collect
repeindre	to repaint
installer	to install
savoir**	to know
connaître**	to know

Had a look ☐ **Nearly there** ☐ **Nailed it** ☐

Les expressions idiomatiques	*Idioms*
pas tellement mon truc!	not really my thing!
ma mission à moi, c'est …	my task is to …
un spectacle son et lumière	a sound and light show

Had a look ☐ **Nearly there** ☐ **Nailed it** ☐

---

*Use *les* + adjective of a region to indicate where a group of people are from.

Examples:
Les Bretons people from Brittany
Les Provençaux people from Provence
Les Lyonnais people from the Lyon region
Les Charentais people from the Charente region

**These two verbs have the same translation but are used in different contexts:

connaître to know people, places, the existence of something and the value of something.
Je connais Lyon, c'est chouette! – I know Lyon, it's great!

savoir to know how to do something, to know information you are aware of and to know of events.
Je sais nager. I know how to swim.

Module 5 Vocabulaire

Words I should know for speaking and writing activities

En vacances	On holiday
l'Algérie (f)	Algeria
l'Allemagne (f)	Germany
l'Angleterre (f)	England
l'Autriche (f)	Austria
la Belgique	Belgium
la Croatie	Croatia
l'Espagne (f)	Spain
les États-Unis (m)	USA
la France	France
le Japon	Japan
le Pakistan	Pakistan
les Pays-Bas (m)	Netherlands
le pays de Galles	Wales
la Pologne	Poland
la Suisse	Switzerland

Had a look ☐   Nearly there ☐   Nailed it ☐

Normalement, je passe mes vacances en/au/à l'/aux … — *Normally, I spend my holidays in …*
Je vais au bord de la mer/à la campagne/à la montagne. — *I go to the seaside/the countryside/the mountains.*
Je voyage en train/avion/ferry/voiture. — *I go by train/plane/ferry/car.*
Je fais du camping. — *I go camping.*
Je loge dans un gîte/un hôtel/chez ma tante. — *I stay in a holiday cottage/a hotel/with my aunt.*
J'y vais avec ma famille/mes grand-parents/mon petit frère. — *I go there with my family/my grandparents/my little brother.*
C'est génial/extra/assez ennuyeux. — *It's great/excellent/quite boring.*
Je me lève tôt. — *I get up early.*
On se couche tard. — *We go to bed late.*
Je me repose/me prépare. — *I rest/get ready.*
Je m'habille. — *I get dressed.*
Je vais à la plage. — *I go to the beach.*
Je me baigne dans la mer. — *I bathe/swim in the sea.*
Je me promène. — *I go for a walk.*
Je rentre à l'hôtel. — *I go back to the hotel.*
Je sors au restaurant. — *I go out to a restaurant.*
On peut … — *You can …*
faire une visite de Paris — *visit Paris*
faire de l'escalade — *go climbing*
visiter les musées/monuments — *visit museums/monuments*
aller à la pêche/à la plage — *go fishing/to the beach*
jouer à la pétanque — *play petanque, boules*

Had a look ☐   Nearly there ☐   Nailed it ☐

Les vacances passées et futures	Holidays past and future
Tous les ans/Normalement/Tous les étés, …	Every year/Normally/Every summer, …
j'achète/je fais/je vais …	I buy/do/go …
Hier/L'année dernière/Le week-end dernier, …	Yesterday/Last year/Last weekend, …
j'ai vu/visité/acheté …	I saw/visited/bought …
je suis allé(e) à …	I went to …
L'année prochaine/Le week-end prochain/Demain, …	Next year/Next weekend/Tomorrow, …
je vais faire/prendre/aller/visiter …	I'm going to do/take/go/visit …

Had a look ☐   Nearly there ☐   Nailed it ☐

Des vacances de rêve	Dream holidays
Je logerais …	I would stay …
dans un gîte à la campagne	in a holiday cottage in the countryside
dans un hôtel 4 étoiles	in a 4-star hotel
dans une auberge de jeunesse	in a youth hostel
dans une caravane	in a caravan
dans une chambre d'hôtes	in a bed and breakfast
dans une tente, sur une île déserte	in a tent on a desert island
sur un bateau	on a boat
Je voyagerais …	I would travel …
avec mes copains/copines	with my friends
avec ma famille	with my family
avec mes parents	with my parents
avec mes grands-parents	with my grandparents
avec mon lycée	with my school
avec une organisation	with an organisation
seul(e)	alone

Had a look ☐   Nearly there ☐   Nailed it ☐

Je regarderais le coucher du soleil. — *I would watch the sunset.*
Je nagerais avec les poissons tropicaux. — *I would swim with tropical fish.*
Je ferais des randonnées. — *I would go hiking.*
Je ferais du canoë-kayak. — *I would go canoeing.*
Je me reposerais. — *I would rest.*
Je m'amuserais avec mes copains/copines. — *I would have fun with my friends.*
Je mangerais bien. — *I would eat well.*

M5

31

Module 5 Vocabulaire

Il y aurait …	There would be …
un café qui serait ouvert toute la nuit	a café which would be open all night
une salle de jeux	a games room
des feux d'artifice tous les soirs	fireworks every night
des spectacles son et lumière	sound and light shows
des visites guidées	guided tours
Il n'y aurait aucun bruit!	There would be no noise!
Il n'y aurait pas beaucoup d'adultes!	There wouldn't be many adults!
Ce serait …	It would be …
formidable	tremendous
luxueux	luxury
merveilleux	wonderful
passionnant	exciting
pittoresque	picturesque
reposant	restful
tranquille	quiet

Had a look ☐ Nearly there ☐ Nailed it ☐

À l'hôtel / At the hotel

Nous avons passé X jours dans cet hôtel/ chambre d'hôte.	We spent X days at this hotel/bed and breakfast
Ça s'est très bien passé.	It all went very well.
C'était charmant/ propre/bien situé.	It was charming/clean/ well located.
très pratique/pas cher/ super	very handy/not expensive/super
Le service était impeccable.	The service was impeccable.
Le Wi-Fi fonctionnait très bien.	The Wi-Fi worked very well.
Le petit-déjeuner était offert.	Breakfast was included.
Il y avait …	There was …
un parking tout près	parking nearby
un micro-onde/la climatisation dans la chambre	a microwave/air-conditioning in the room
Il y avait un très bon rapport qualité-prix.	It was very good value for money.
Nous y avons passé un super séjour.	We had a super stay there.

Had a look ☐ Nearly there ☐ Nailed it ☐

French	English
Je voudrais une chambre …	I would like a room …
pour une personne	for one person
pour deux personnes	for two people
avec un lit simple	with a single bed
avec un grand lit	with a double bed
avec une salle de bains	with a bathroom
avec une douche	with a shower
avec une vue sur la mer	with a sea view
Votre chambre est …	Your room is …
au rez-de-chaussée	on the ground floor
au premier/deuxième étage	on the first/second floor

Had a look ☐ Nearly there ☐ Nailed it ☐

Au restaurant / At the restaurant

Je préférerais une table …	I would prefer a table …
en terrasse/à l'intérieur	on the terrace/inside
Je vais prendre …	I will have/take …
le plat du jour/le menu à 30 euros	the dish of the day/the 30 euros set menu
(la soupe à la tomate) en entrée	(the tomato soup) for a starter
(le filet de loup de mer) comme plat principal	(the fillet of seabass) for the main course
(la mousse au chocolat) comme dessert	(the chocolate mousse) for dessert
Qu'est-ce que vous avez, comme desserts?	What desserts do you have?
On peut avoir l'addition, s'il vous plaît?	Could we have the bill, please?

Had a look ☐ Nearly there ☐ Nailed it ☐

Les prix n'étaient pas excessifs.	The prices weren't excessive.
C'était cher.	It was expensive.
L'accueil était très chaleureux.	The welcome was very warm.
Nous avons dû attendre plus de cinq minutes.	We had to wait more than five minutes.
L'ambiance était vraiment agréable.	The ambiance was really pleasant.
L'atmosphère était super bruyante.	The atmosphere was very noisy.
Le serveur/La serveuse était …	The waiter/waitress was …
très attentionné(e)/ médiocre	very attentive/mediocre
À recommander!	To be recommended!
Je n'y retournerai jamais!	I will never go back there!
un couteau	a knife
une cuillère	a spoon
une fourchette	a fork
une serviette	a napkin

Had a look ☐ Nearly there ☐ Nailed it ☐

Les plats / The dishes

les entrées (f)	starters
les brochettes (f) de crevettes (f)	prawn skewers
les escargots (m)	snails
la soupe à la tomate	tomato soup

Module 5 Vocabulaire

la tarte à l'oignon	onion tart	Que penses-tu de (cette théière)?	What do you think of (this teapot)?
les plats principaux (m)	main dishes	Je crois que je vais acheter (ces bijoux).	I think I'm going to buy (this jewellery).
l'épaule (f) d'agneau	lamb shoulder	Je veux acheter (un foulard).	I want to buy (a scarf).
la cuisse de canard	duck leg		
le gratin dauphinois	dauphinoise potatoes	Tu préfères celui-ci ou celui-là?	Do you prefer this one or that one?
les lasagnes (f) végétariennes	vegetarian lasagne	Je cherche (une lanterne) pour (ma sœur).	I'm looking for (a lantern) for (my sister).
le loup de mer	sea bass		
le poulet basquaise	Basque-style chicken	Je prends celle-ci ou celle-là?	Shall I take this one or that one?
le rôti de veau	roast veal		
les desserts (m)	desserts	J'ai envie de m'acheter des (gants).	I feel like buying some (gloves).
la crème brûlée	crème brûlée		
la mousse au chocolat	chocolate mousse	Tu trouves celles-ci comment?	What do you think of these?
le roulé au chocolat	chocolate roll		
le sorbet	sorbet	Je déteste faire du shopping.	I hate going shopping.
la tarte au citron	lemon tart		
la tarte aux pommes	apple tart	Je suis accro au shopping.	I'm addicted to shopping.

Had a look ☐ Nearly there ☐ Nailed it ☐

Had a look ☐ Nearly there ☐ Nailed it ☐

En route! / On the road!

Si j'avais le choix, pour aller …	If I had the choice, to go …
en Inde/Russie/Chine	to India/Russia/China
au Sénégal/Vietnam/Brésil	to Senegal/Vietnam/Brazil
… je voyagerais …	… I would travel …
en car/train/avion	by coach/train/plane
à moto	by motorbike
… car c'est/ce n'est pas …	… because it is (not) …
rapide/confortable/pratique	quick/comfortable/practical
une aventure/la classe	an adventure/cool
bon pour l'environnement	good for the environment
ennuyeux	boring
fatigant	tiring
cher	expensive
un billet	a ticket
un aller simple	a single
un aller-retour	a return
en première classe	in first class
en deuxième classe	in second class
les horaires	travel time(s)
le guichet	ticket office
le quai	platform
la salle d'attente	waiting room

C'était catastrophique! / It was catastrophic!

Avant de partir, j'avais …	Before leaving I had …
réservé mon billet d'avion	booked my plane ticket
fait ma valise/des recherches	packed my case/done some research
découvert/décidé que …	discovered/decided that …
tout préparé	prepared everything
J'étais allé(e) à l'agence de voyages.	I had gone to the travel agent's.
Mais/Pourtant …	But/However …
je me suis cassé la jambe	I broke my leg
j'ai oublié mon passeport	I forgot my passport
j'ai raté l'avion	I missed the plane
j'ai pris un coup de soleil affreux	I got terribly sunburnt
le camping-car est tombé en panne	the camper van broke down
on m'a volé mon sac à main	my handbag was stolen
Alors/Donc …	So …
j'ai dû aller au commissariat/à l'hôpital/chez le médecin	I had to go to the police station/hospital/doctor's
Quelle horreur!	How awful!
J'étais triste.	I was sad.
On était bien déçus.	We were really disappointed.

Had a look ☐ Nearly there ☐ Nailed it ☐

Acheter les souvenirs / Buying souvenirs

Je pense acheter (ce tagine).	I'm thinking of buying (this tagine).
Qu'est-ce que tu en penses?	What do you think of it?

Had a look ☐ Nearly there ☐ Nailed it ☐

Module 5 Vocabulaire

Extra words I should know for reading and listening activities

Les souvenirs de vacances	*Holiday memories*
le tagine	Moroccan cooking pot
la théière	teapot
les poissons tropicaux (m)	tropical fish
les créatures (f)	creatures

Had a look ☐ Nearly there ☐ Nailed it ☐

En vacances	*On holiday!*
les vacances de neige (f)	winter holidays
l'île déserte (f)	desert island
le coin de paradis	corner of paradise
dans un beau cadre	in a beautiful area
à l'intérieur	inside
le parc naturel	nature/national park
le coup de soleil	sunburn
les marchands (m)	shopkeepers
l'auberge de jeunesse (f)	youth hostel
la climatisation	air-conditioning
le pourboire	tip
l'hôtel 4 étoiles (m)	4 star hotel
la formule demi-pension	half-board
en montgolfière (f)	in a hot air ballon
le Wi-Fi	wi-fi

Had a look ☐ Nearly there ☐ Nailed it ☐

Les activités de vacances	*Holiday activities*
installer	to put in
emporter	to take
vomir	to be sick
être à couper le souffle	to be breath-taking
profiter de	to make the most of
se baigner	to swim
endormir	to fall asleep
rater	to miss (bus, etc.)
faire des recherches	to research
rapporter	to bring back
essayer	to try
tomber en panne	to break down
voler	to steal
hurler	to scream
loger	to stay
en regardant …	while watching …

Had a look ☐ Nearly there ☐ Nailed it ☐

Les expressions idiomatiques	*Idioms*
c'est une bonne affaire?	is it a good deal/bargain?
qu'est-que c'était cher!	it was so expensive!
chez le médecin	at the doctor's
à recommander!	I would recommend it!
le petit-déjeuner était offert!*	breakfast was included!

Had a look ☐ Nearly there ☐ Nailed it ☐

> ⭐ *Offert* really means 'offered' but it conveys the idea of 'given away with' something, so here breakfast is given away with the stay in the hotel!
>
> Another example:
>
> *Achetez deux jeux et le troisième est offert!* Buy two games and the third is free/given away!

Module 6 Vocabulaire

Words I should know for speaking and writing activities

Les matières	*School subjects*
le commerce	*business studies*
le dessin	*art*
les arts plastiques (m)	*fine art*
le français	*French*
le latin	*Latin*
la biologie/les sciences de la vie et de la terre	*biology*
la chimie	*chemistry*
la géographie	*geography*
la musique	*music*
la physique/les sciences physiques	*physics*
la religion	*religious studies*
la sociologie	*sociology*
la technologie	*design and technology*
l'allemand (m)	*German*
l'anglais (m)	*English*

Had a look ☐ **Nearly there** ☐ **Nailed it** ☐

l'art dramatique (m)	*drama*
l'économie (f)	*economics*
l'éducation physique et sportive/l'EPS (f)	*PE*
l'espagnol (m)	*Spanish*
l'étude des médias (f)	*media studies*
l'histoire (f)	*history*
l'histoire-géo (f)	*humanities (history and geography, studied together in France)*
l'informatique (f)	*ICT*
l'instruction civique (f)	*citizenship*
l'italien (m)	*Italian*
les arts ménagers (m)	*home technology*
les maths (f)	*maths*

Had a look ☐ **Nearly there** ☐ **Nailed it** ☐

Mon collège / *My school*

Mercredi, à 11h15, j'ai histoire-géo.	*I have humanities at 11:15 a.m. on Wednesday.*
J'ai (deux) heures de (musique) par semaine.	*I have (two) hours of (music) per week.*
Il n'y a pas de cours de … dans mon emploi du temps.	*There are no … lessons in my timetable.*
J'apprends (deux) langues vivantes.	*I learn (two) foreign languages.*
Mes cours finissent à (16h00) tous les jours.	*My lessons finish at (4:00 p.m.) every day.*
Je n'ai pas cours (le mercredi après-midi).	*I don't have lessons (on Wednesday afternoon).*
Ma matière préférée est …	*My favourite subject is …*
J'adore/j'aime/je n'aime pas/je déteste …	*I love/like/don't like/hate …*

Je trouve …	*I find …*
Je pense que … est/sont …	*I think that … is …*
intéressant(e)(s)	*interesting*
passionnant(e)(s)	*exciting*
ennuyeux/-euse(s)	*boring*
… parce que/qu' …	*… because …*
c'est facile/fascinant/difficile/utile/inutile	*it's easy/fascinating/difficult/useful/useless*
Je suis fort(e)/faible/doué(e) en …	*I am strong/weak/gifted in …*
Le/La prof est bon(ne)/sympa/marrant(e)/sévère/gentil(le)/impatient(e).	*The teacher is good/nice/funny/strict/kind/impatient.*
On a trop de devoirs.	*We have too much homework.*

Had a look ☐ **Nearly there** ☐ **Nailed it** ☐

Mon bahut / *My school*

Comment s'appelle ton collège?	*What's your school called?*
Mon collège s'appelle …	*My school is called …*
C'est quelle sorte de collège?	*What sort of school is it?*
C'est un collège mixte pour les élèves de onze à seize ans.	*It's a mixed school for pupils from 11 to 16.*
Il y a combien d'élèves?	*How many pupils are there?*
Il y a 750 élèves et quarante-cinq professeurs.	*There are 750 pupils and 45 teachers.*
Quelles sont les horaires du collège?	*What are the school hours?*
Les cours commencent à 8h30.	*Lessons start at 8:30 a.m.*
La récré est à 10h15 et dure quinze minutes.	*Break is at 10:15 a.m. and lasts 15 minutes.*
On a une heure et demie pour le déjeuner.	*We have an hour and a half for lunch.*
Les cours finissent à 16 heures.	*Lessons finish at 4:00 p.m.*

Had a look ☐ **Nearly there** ☐ **Nailed it** ☐

Il y a combien de cours par jour?	*How many lessons are there per day?*
Il y a sept cours de cinquante-cinq minutes par jour.	*There are seven lessons of 55 minutes per day.*
Le mercredi après-midi, il n'y a pas cours.	*There are no lessons on Wednesday afternoon.*
Quelles matières étudies-tu?	*What subjects do you study?*

M6

35

Module 6 Vocabulaire

French	English
J'étudie douze matières dont …	I study 12 subjects, including …
Toutes mes matières sont obligatoires.	All my subjects are compulsory.
Quelle est ta matière préférée?	What is your favourite subject?

Had a look ☐ **Nearly there** ☐ **Nailed it** ☐

Ma matière préférée, c'est (les arts ménagers) car …	My favourite subject is (home technology) because …
J'adore (cuisiner) car … je suis doué(e) pour ça	I love (cooking) because … I'm talented at that
Comment sont les professeurs?	What are your teachers like?
Les profs sont sympa/sévères.	The teachers are nice/strict.
Qu'est-ce que tu penses de ton collège?	What do you think of your school?
Je trouve que/qu' …	I find that …
les journées sont trop longues	the days are too long
on a trop de contrôles	we have too many tests
les profs sont excellents	the teachers are excellent

Had a look ☐ **Nearly there** ☐ **Nailed it** ☐

L'école chez nous, l'école chez vous / *School here and with you*

French	English
En Angleterre/Écosse/Irlande du Nord …	In England/Scotland/Northern Ireland …
Au pays de Galles …	In Wales …
on va à l'école de … ans à … ans	we go to school from … to … years old
l'école commence à … heures et finit à … heures	school starts at … and finishes at …
on porte un uniforme scolaire/ses propres vêtements	we wear a school uniform/our own clothes
on achète ses propres stylos et règles	we buy our own pens and rulers
on ne redouble pas	we don't repeat the year
on étudie …	we study …
Mais en France/au Canada/au Mali …	But in France/Canada/Mali …
ils vont …	they go …
l'école commence …	school starts …
ils portent …	they wear …
ils achètent …	they buy …
ils (ne) redoublent (pas)	they (don't) repeat the year
ils étudient …	they study …
Je préfère le système (anglais/français)	I prefer the (English/French) system
parce que …	because …
les horaires sont plus raisonnables	the hours are more sensible

French	English
l'uniforme scolaire est pratique/inutile	school uniform is practical/useless
l'école fournit l'équipement	school provides the equipment
le redoublement (n')est (pas) une bonne idée	repeating the year is (not) a good idea
on (n')étudie (pas) …	we/they (don't) study …

Had a look ☐ **Nearly there** ☐ **Nailed it** ☐

Le règlement scolaire / *School rules*

French	English
Dans cette école, il faut …	In this school, you must …
être à l'heure	be on time
faire ses devoirs	do your homework
porter l'uniforme scolaire	wear school uniform
Il ne faut pas …	You must not …
manquer les cours	miss lessons
tricher pendant un contrôle	cheat in a test
Il est interdit de/d' …	It is forbidden to …
mâcher du chewing-gum	chew gum
utiliser son portable en classe	use your mobile in class
porter des bijoux/des piercings/trop de maquillage	wear jewellery/piercings/too much make-up
harceler d'autres élèves	bully other pupils
sortir de l'école pendant l'heure du déjeuner	leave school during the lunch hour

Had a look ☐ **Nearly there** ☐ **Nailed it** ☐

French	English
Je trouve ça …	I find that …
raisonnable	reasonable, sensible
logique	logical
juste/injuste	fair/unfair
ridicule/frustrant	ridiculous/frustrating
… parce que/car …	… because …
c'est/ce n'est pas dangereux	it's (not) dangerous
il faut protéger les jeunes	you must protect young people
on n'est pas des bébés	we're not babies
il faut respecter les autres	you must respect others
la mode n'a pas de place à l'école	fashion has no place at school
c'est/ce n'est pas important	it's (not) important
l'école, c'est pour apprendre	school is for learning
J'ai eu une heure de retenue/de colle.	I had an hour of detention.
J'ai dû copier des lignes.	I had to write lines.

Had a look ☐ **Nearly there** ☐ **Nailed it** ☐

Module 6 Vocabulaire

Quelle perte de temps!	What a waste of time!
Je pense que tu as raison.	I think you're right.
Ah non, tu as tort.	Oh no, you're wrong.
Moi aussi, je trouve que …	Me too, I find that …
Je (ne) suis (pas) d'accord avec toi.	I (don't) agree with you.
Tu rigoles!	You're joking!

Had a look ☐ Nearly there ☐ Nailed it ☐

Profiter de l'école / *Making the most of school*

Présentez-vous pour être délégué(e) de classe.	Put yourself forward to be class representative.
Levez la main autant que possible en classe.	Raise your hand as often as possible in class.
Participez à la chorale.	Join the choir.
Soyez «écolo».	Be 'green'.
N'ayez pas peur de remettre en cause les attitudes sexistes, racistes ou homophobes.	Don't be afraid to challenge sexist, racist or homophobic attitudes.
Faites une activité sportive.	Do a sporting activity.
N'oubliez pas de remercier vos profs.	Don't forget to thank your teachers.
Soyez gentils avec les plus jeunes.	Be kind to the youngest ones.
Profitez des sorties scolaires.	Make the most of your school trips.
Amusez-vous bien!	Have lots of fun!

Had a look ☐ Nearly there ☐ Nailed it ☐

C'est quoi, ton plus grand accomplissement au collège?	What is your greatest achievement at school?
Je joue dans l'équipe de rugby.	I play in the rugby team.
Je représente les opinions de mes camarades de classe.	I put forward my classmates' opinions.
Je n'oublierai jamais cette expérience.	I will never forget this experience.
Je fais partie du club de théâtre.	I am in the drama club.
C'est une bonne préparation pour la vie d'adulte.	It's good preparation for adult life.
Je suis fier/-ière car je n'ai pas beaucoup confiance en moi.	I am proud because I don't have much self-confidence.

Ce succès est mérité car je travaille très dur.	I deserve my success because I work hard.
J'ai donné un concert.	I gave a concert.
J'ai toujours de bons commentaires sur mon bulletin scolaire.	I always get good comments in my school report.
C'est un honneur de représenter son école.	It's an honour to represent your school.

Had a look ☐ Nearly there ☐ Nailed it ☐

En échange / *On an exchange*

Pourquoi faire un échange scolaire?	Why go on a school exchange?
On se fait de nouveaux amis.	You make new friends.
On améliore ses compétences en langue.	You improve your language skills.
On habite chez une famille d'une culture différente.	You live with a family from another culture.
On visite un nouveau pays ou une nouvelle région.	You visit a new country or region.
On apprécie non seulement les différences mais aussi les similarités entre nos vies.	You appreciate not only the differences, but also the similarities between our lives.

Had a look ☐ Nearly there ☐ Nailed it ☐

Mon/Ma correspondant(e) anglais(e) est arrivé(e) il y a (cinq) jours.	My English exchange partner arrived (five) days ago.
Les élèves et leurs profs sont arrivés (en car).	The pupils and their teachers arrived (by coach).
J'ai été content(e) de rencontrer X.	I was pleased to meet X.
On a passé le premier week-end en famille.	We spent the first weekend with the family.
Nous sommes allés au collège ensemble.	We went to school together.
Nous avons visité …	We visited …
On a participé à …	We took part in …
Il y aura une sortie à …	There will be an outing to …

Had a look ☐ Nearly there ☐ Nailed it ☐

M 6

Module 6 Vocabulaire

Extra words I should know for reading and listening activities

Les personnes	People
le/la surveillant(e)	supervisor
l'internat (m)	boarding school
le/la collégien(ne)	high school student (up to yr10)
le/la correspondant(e)	penfriend

Had a look ☐ **Nearly there** ☐ **Nailed it** ☐

Les activités au collège	School activities
les arts plastiques (m)	fine arts
la musculation	body building
l'entraînement (m)	training
l'instruction civique (f)	citizenship
le progrès	progress
la maternelle	pre-school, nursery school
le bac	A levels
le contrôle	test
la pièce de théâtre	play
la chorale	choir
la marche rapide	power-walking
le chant	singing
le sommeil	sleep
la scolarité	schooling
la mémoire	memory
les compétences (f)	skills

Had a look ☐ **Nearly there** ☐ **Nailed it** ☐

Les problèmes au collège	School problems
sécher les cours/ manquer les cours	to skip lessons/to truant
en quittant …	on leaving …
mâcher	to chew
harceler	to bully
tricher	to cheat
stresser	to stress
améliorer	to improve

Had a look ☐ **Nearly there** ☐ **Nailed it** ☐

Comment faire bonne impression?	How do you make a good impression?
autant que possible	as often as possible
combattre la discrimination	to fight discrimination
trier correctement ce que vous jetez	to sort out correctly what you throw away

Had a look ☐ **Nearly there** ☐ **Nailed it** ☐

L'avenir	The future
Je quitterai mon collège.	I will leave my middle/ high school.
J'ai l'intention de + infinitive …	I intend to …
Je me présenterai à l'élection.	I will stand in the election.
Je jouerai au hand.	I will play handball.
J'écrirai des articles.	I will write some articles.
Je verrai des films.	I will watch some films.
Je continuerai à + infinitive …	I will keep/continue to …
fin juin	at the end of June
en ce moment	at the moment
l'année prochaine	next year
avoir de bonnes/ mauvaises notes	to have good/bad marks
être bien dans sa peau*	to feel good about yourself

Had a look ☐ **Nearly there** ☐ **Nailed it** ☐

> ⭐ *Break unfamiliar idioms down into their component parts to work out their meaning:
>
> être bien dans sa peau: être bien + dans sa peau
> to be well + in one's skin (to feel comfortable in your own skin or to feel good about yourself).

Module 7 Vocabulaire

Words I should know for speaking and writing activities

Les professions / Jobs

Ma mère/Mon père est …	My mum/dad is a(n) …
Je voudrais être …	I would like to be a(n) …
acteur/-rice	actor/actress
agent de police	policeman/woman
agriculteur/-rice	farmer
architecte	architect
boucher/-ère	butcher
boulanger/-ère	baker
caissier/-ère	cashier
coiffeur/-euse	hairdresser
créateur/-rice de mode	fashion designer
dentiste	dentist
directeur/-rice	director
électricien(ne)	electrician
employé(e) de bureau	office worker

Had a look ☐ **Nearly there** ☐ **Nailed it** ☐

French	English
facteur/-rice	postman/postwoman
fonctionnaire	civil servant
infirmier/-ère	nurse
informaticien(ne)	computer scientist
ingénieur(e)	engineer
journaliste	journalist
maçon(ne)	builder
mécanicien(ne)	mechanic
médecin	doctor
professeur	teacher
secrétaire	secretary
serveur/-euse	waiter/waitress
soldat	soldier
steward/hôtesse de l'air	flight attendant
vendeur/-euse	sales assistant
vétérinaire	vet

Had a look ☐ **Nearly there** ☐ **Nailed it** ☐

French	English
J'adore (la campagne).	I love (the countryside).
Je suis passionné(e) par (la loi et la justice).	I'm passionate about (the law and justice).
Je suis fort(e) en (maths).	I'm good at (maths).
Je suis (courageux/-euse).	I am (brave).
(Voyager), c'est ma passion.	(Travelling) is my passion.
(Les avions) me fascinent.	(Planes) fascinate me.
Je préférerais travailler (en plein air).	I would prefer to work (outdoors).
Je voudrais travailler avec (des enfants).	I would like to work with (children).
Je voudrais/J'aimerais travailler comme …	I would like to work as …
Je veux être …	I want to be …

Had a look ☐ **Nearly there** ☐ **Nailed it** ☐

L'orientation / Career paths

Dans quel secteur voudrais-tu travailler?	In which area would you like to work?
l'audiovisuel et les médias	audiovisual and media
l'informatique et les télécommunications	IT and telecommunications
l'hôtellerie et la restauration	hotel and catering
les arts et la culture	arts and culture
le commerce	business
le sport et les loisirs	sport and leisure
la médecine et la santé	medicine and health
les sciences et les technologies	science and technology
Ça m'intéresserait de travailler dans …	I would be interested in working in …
Mon rêve serait de faire carrière dans …	My dream would be to have a career in …
Mon ambition/Mon but est de trouver un poste dans …	My ambition/aim is to find a job in …

Had a look ☐ **Nearly there** ☐ **Nailed it** ☐

French	English
Le secteur/L'orientation qui m'attire/m'intéresse (le plus), c'est …	The sector/career path that attracts/interests me (the most) is …
L'important pour moi est d'avoir un métier bien payé.	The important thing for me is to have a well-paid job.
Le plus important est de …	The most important thing is to …
faire quelque chose de satisfaisant/stimulant/ gratifiant/d'intéressant	do something satisfying/ stimulating/rewarding/ interesting
faire quelque chose pour améliorer la société/aider les autres	do something to improve society/help others
Le salaire a moins d'importance/est très important pour moi.	The salary is less/very important to me.
À mon avis, c'est un secteur d'avenir.	In my opinion, it's an area with prospects.
Je suis … depuis (trois) ans.	I have been a … for (three) years.
C'est un métier (stimulant).	It's a (stimulating) job.

Had a look ☐ **Nearly there** ☐ **Nailed it** ☐

French	English
La chose qui me plaît le plus, c'est …	What I like best is …
L'inconvénient, c'est que …	The disadvantage is that …
les horaires sont très longs	the hours are very long

M7

39

Module 7 Vocabulaire

French	English
c'est fatigant	it's tiring
Le mieux/pire, c'est …	The best/worst thing is …
Je suis assez satisfait(e) de mon travail.	I'm quite satisfied with my job.
Avant, j'étais/je travaillais comme …	In the past, I was/worked as …
C'était affreux/stressant/mieux/pire.	It was awful/stressful/better/worse.
C'était mal payé.	It was badly paid.
Le travail était monotone.	The work was monotonous.
Il n'y avait aucune possibilité d'avancement.	There was no chance of promotion.
Je m'entendais mal avec mon patron.	I didn't get on well with my boss.
J'ai décidé de (suivre une formation).	I decided to (take a course).
Maintenant, je suis diplômé(e).	Now I am qualified.
Mon nouveau boulot est (plus créatif).	My new job is (more creative).
Mes collègues sont tous très sympa.	My colleagues are all very nice.

Had a look ☐   Nearly there ☐   Nailed it ☐

Les ambitions / *Ambitions*

French	English
Avant de continuer mes études, …	Before I continue my studies …
Après avoir terminé mes examens, …	After having finished my exams …
Après avoir quitté le collège, …	After having left school …
Plus tard/Un jour, …	Later on/One day …
Je veux/J'aimerais/Je préférerais/J'espère	I want/I would like/I would prefer/I hope
J'ai envie de/d' …	I want to …
J'ai l'intention de/d' …	I intend to …
Mon rêve serait de/d' …	My dream would be to …
aller à l'université/à la fac	go to university
entrer en apprentissage	do an apprenticeship
faire du bénévolat/travail bénévole	do charity/voluntary work
prendre une année sabbatique	take a gap year
J'espère me marier/me pacser.	I hope to get married/register a civil partnership.
J'ai l'intention de faire le tour du monde.	I intend to travel round the world.
Mon but est de fonder une famille.	My aim is to start a family.
Je ne veux pas avoir d'enfants.	I don't want to have children.
Je n'ai aucune intention de m'installer avec mon copain/ma copine.	I have no intention of moving in with my boyfriend/girlfriend.

Had a look ☐   Nearly there ☐   Nailed it ☐

Les langues / *Languages*

French	English
Tu parles quelles langues?	Which languages do you speak?
Je parle bien/couramment/un peu/mal …	I speak … well/fluently/a bit/badly.
Je me débrouille en …	I get by in …
Ma mère parle …	My mother speaks …
Mon beau-père se débrouille en …	My stepfather gets by in …
Actuellement, ma sœur apprend …	Currently, my sister is learning …

Had a look ☐   Nearly there ☐   Nailed it ☐

French	English
l'allemand (m)	German
l'anglais (m)	English
l'arabe (m)	Arabic
le français	French
l'espagnol (m)	Spanish
l'italien (m)	Italian
le japonais	Japanese
le mandarin	Mandarin
le portugais	Portuguese
le russe	Russian
Mon frère ne parle aucune langue étrangère.	My brother doesn't speak any foreign languages.
Ma grand-mère parle seulement le hindi.	My grandmother only speaks Hindi.

Had a look ☐   Nearly there ☐   Nailed it ☐

French	English
évidemment	obviously
actuellement	currently
naturellement	naturally, of course
vraiment	really
seulement	only
bien	well
mal	badly
mieux	better
Savoir parler des langues …	Knowing how to speak languages …
est indispensable pour certaines professions	is indispensable for certain jobs
ne sert à rien pour d'autres	is of no use for others
donne plus de possibilités de carrière	provides more career opportunities
est un atout	is an asset
On peut trouver plus facilement un bon emploi dans un autre pays.	You can find a job more easily in another country.
On comprend mieux sa propre langue.	You understand your own language better.

Module 7 Vocabulaire

French	English
On a plus de chances d'obtenir une promotion.	You have more chance of promotion.
On peut mieux connaître les gens et la culture d'un pays.	You can get to know the people and culture of a country better.
On peut voyager/se faire des amis partout dans le monde.	You can travel/make friends all over the world.

Had a look ☐ **Nearly there** ☐ **Nailed it** ☐

Au téléphone / On the telephone

French	English
Allô?	Hello?
Je voudrais parler avec …	I would like to talk to …
Sa ligne est occupée.	His/Her line is busy.
Est-ce que je peux laisser un message?	Can I leave a message?
Je vais vous transférer vers sa messagerie vocale.	I will transfer you to his/her voicemail.
Ne quittez pas.	Stay on the line.
Je vous le passe.	I'll pass you over to him/her.
Je peux vous être utile?	Can I help you/be of help?
Au revoir!	Goodbye!

Had a look ☐ **Nearly there** ☐ **Nailed it** ☐

Un entretien d'embauche / A job interview

French	English
Enchanté(e).	Pleased to meet you.
Asseyez-vous.	Sit down.
Parlez-moi un peu de ce que vous faites actuellement.	Talk to me a little bit about what you are doing at the moment.
Actuellement, je suis (au lycée).	At the moment, I am (in sixth form college).
Je suis en train de (préparer le baccalauréat/mes examens de GCSE).	I am in the middle of (preparing to take my baccalauréat/my GCSE exams).
Quelles matières étudiez-vous?	What subjects are you studying?
J'étudie (huit) matières, dont (l'EPS).	I'm studying (eight) subjects, including (PE).
Qu'est-ce que vous ferez après vos examens?	What will you do after your exams?
Si je réussis mes examens, j'espère (aller à l'université).	If I pass my exams, I hope (to go to university).
J'aimerais également (prendre une année sabbatique).	I would also like (to take a gap year).
Pourquoi vous intéressez-vous à ce poste?	Why are you interested in this position?
Je crois que ce serait une bonne expérience pour moi.	I think it would be a good experience for me.
Quelles sont les qualités personnelles que vous apporteriez à ce poste?	What personal qualities would you bring to this position?
Je suis quelqu'un de (bien organisé/de très motivé/de créatif).	I am a (well organised/ very motivated/creative) person.

Had a look ☐ **Nearly there** ☐ **Nailed it** ☐

Mon boulot dans le tourisme / My job in tourism

French	English
Je suis étudiant(e) en …	I am studying …
J'apprends à devenir …	I'm learning to become …
Il y a six mois, j'ai commencé à travailler dans/chez/en …	Six months ago I started work in/with …
Je voudrais travailler à plein temps dans (le tourisme).	I would like to work full-time in (tourism).
Lorsque j'étais plus jeune, je rêvais d'être (infirmier/-ière).	When I was younger, I dreamed of being a (nurse).
J'ai décidé de changer d'orientation à cause de …	I decided to change direction because of …
Mon travail consiste à (accueillir les clients).	My work involves (welcoming clients).
Je m'occupe aussi (des réservations).	I also take care of (reservations).

Had a look ☐ **Nearly there** ☐ **Nailed it** ☐

French	English
Je vends (des billets).	I sell (tickets).
Je suis passionné(e) par mon travail.	I am passionate about my job.
J'apprécie surtout (le contact avec les gens).	I particularly enjoy (dealing with people).
Le seul inconvénient de mon métier, c'est que …	The only disadvantage of my job is that …
Pour faire ce métier, il faut …	To do this job you have to …
être souriant	smile
savoir parler d'autres langues	know how to speak other languages
Plus tard/Quand je serai diplômé(e), …	Later on/When I am qualified …
je partirai en vacances	I will go on holiday
j'essaierai d'apprendre le japonais	I will try to learn Japanese

Had a look ☐ **Nearly there** ☐ **Nailed it** ☐

Extra words I should know for reading and listening activities

Le travail	Work
l'hôtellerie (f)	hotel business
la restauration	catering
l'orientation (f)	careers advice
l'horaire (m)	timetable
la possibilité	possibility
la formation	training
le boulot	job
l'année sabbatique (f)	sabbatical, gap year
la licence	degree
la sécurité	security
le respect	respect
la maîtrise	expertise
l'inconvénient (m)	disadvantage
la lettre de motivation	covering letter
l'encadrement (m)	training
la fac	uni

Had a look ☐ Nearly there ☐ Nailed it ☐

Les descriptions des emplois	Work-related descriptions
diplômé(e)	qualified
stimulant(e)	stimulating
ancien(ne)*	former, ancient
pire	worse
mal payé(e)	badly paid
monotone	monotonous
affreux/-euse	awful
enrichissant(e)	enriching
de mauvaise humeur	in a bad mood
créatif/-ve	creative
autonome	independent
apprenti(e)	trainee, apprentice
moi-même	myself
à plein temps	full-time

Had a look ☐ Nearly there ☐ Nailed it ☐

Les activités au travail	Work-related activities
se débrouiller	to cope, to manage
garantir	to guarantee
remplir	to fill
s'adapter à	to adapt to

⭐ *Remember that some adjectives like *ancien* change their meaning depending on where they go in relation to the noun.

Examples:

un ancien collège a former school

une ville ancienne an ancient town

s'organiser	to get organised
entraîner	to train
accueillir	to welcome
prendre en charge	to take charge
animer	to lead/facilitate activities
s'occuper de	to look after
garder les enfants	to babysit
Que faire?	What do I do?
poser sa candidature	to apply for (a job)
après avoir/être + past participle**	after having …

Had a look ☐ Nearly there ☐ Nailed it ☐

Les langues qu'on parle	The languages that we speak
Il/Elle en parle six!	He/She speaks six of them!
les paroles	words
la langue des signes	sign language
Il/Elle a étudié une langue à la fac.	He/She studied a language at uni.
savoir parler	to know how to speak
une autre langue	another language
pouvoir parler	to be able to speak
une langue étrangère	a foreign language
sa propre langue	your own language
plusieurs langues	several languages
communiquer avec des gens	to communicate with people
trouver facilement un bon emploi	to find a good job easily
voyager	to travel
travailler dans des entreprises internationales	to work in international companies
les métiers	professions

Had a look ☐ Nearly there ☐ Nailed it ☐

⭐ **Use this structure to add a different dimension to your phrases in the past tense.

Example:

Après avoir posé ma candidature … After having applied for the job …

Remember to agree the past participle with the subject when using *être*.

Example:

Après être rentrée à la maison, la femme a ouvert les fenêtres. After having returned home, the woman opened the windows.

Module 8 Vocabulaire

Words I should know for speaking and writing activities

Ce qui me préoccupe / *What worries me*

Ce qui est important pour moi dans la vie, c'est d'abord …	*The most important thing to me in life is above all …*
Ensuite, c'est …	*Then it's …*
le sport	*sport*
la musique	*music*
ma santé	*my health*
ma famille	*my family*
l'argent (m)	*money*
mes études	*my studies*
mes animaux	*my pets*
mes amis	*my friends*
Ce qui me préoccupe/ m'inquiète (le plus), c'est …	*What worries me (the most) is …*
l'état (m) de la Terre	*the state of the Earth*
le réchauffement climatique	*global warming*
la pauvreté dans le monde	*world poverty*
l'injustice (f)	*injustice*
l'environnement (m)	*the environment*
les sans-abri	*homeless people*
les personnes qui sont emprisonnées à tort	*people who have been wrongly imprisoned*
les enfants qui n'ont pas à manger	*starving children*

Had a look ☐ **Nearly there** ☐ **Nailed it** ☐

On peut/Il est possible de …	*You can/It's possible to …*
parrainer un enfant en Afrique	*sponsor a child in Africa*
faire un don à une association caritative	*donate to a charity*
faire du bénévolat	*do voluntary work*
Il faut …	*We must …*
lutter contre la faim	*fight against hunger/ famine*
lancer des pétitions	*launch petitions*
écrire à son/sa député(e)	*write to our MP*
participer à des manifestations	*take part in demonstrations*
agir maintenant	*act now*
faire des campagnes de sensibilisation	*carry out campaigns to raise awareness*
Il ne faut pas ignorer (ces gens).	*We must not ignore (these people).*

Had a look ☐ **Nearly there** ☐ **Nailed it** ☐

Notre planète / *Our planet*

Le plus grand problème pour la planète, c'est …	*The greatest problem for the planet is …*
le changement climatique	*climate change*
le déboisement	*deforestation*
la destruction de la couche d'ozone	*the destruction of the ozone layer*
la destruction des forêts tropicales	*the destruction of tropical rainforests*
la disparition des espèces	*species dying out*
la guerre	*war*
le manque d'eau douce	*the lack of fresh water*
la pollution de l'air	*air pollution*
la sécheresse	*drought*
la surpopulation	*overpopulation*
un incendie (m)	*a fire*
une fuite de pétrole	*an oil spill*
des inondations (f)	*flooding, floods*
un tremblement de terre	*an earthquake*
un typhon	*a typhoon*

Had a look ☐ **Nearly there** ☐ **Nailed it** ☐

Protéger l'environnement / *Protecting the environment*

Que devrait-on faire pour sauver notre planète?	*What should we do to save our planet?*
Actuellement, je ne fais pas grand-chose pour protéger l'environnement.	*Currently, I don't do much to protect the environment.*
Je fais déjà pas mal de choses.	*I already do quite a lot.*
Je pourrais/On devrait …	*I could/We ought to …*
trier les déchets	*separate the rubbish*
faire du compost à la maison	*make compost at home*
éteindre les appareils électriques et la lumière en quittant une pièce	*turn off appliances and the light when leaving a room*
baisser le chauffage et mettre un pull	*turn down the heating and put on a sweater*
utiliser du papier recyclé	*use recycled paper*
éviter les produits jetables	*avoid disposable products*
acheter des produits verts	*buy green products*

Had a look ☐ **Nearly there** ☐ **Nailed it** ☐

Module 8 Vocabulaire

privilégier les produits bio	where possible, choose organic products
utiliser les transports en commun	use public transport
favoriser le covoiturage	encourage car-sharing
aller au collège à vélo	go to school by bike
refuser les sacs en plastique	turn down plastic bags
apporter une bouteille d'eau au lieu de prendre un gobelet jetable	carry a bottle of water instead of using disposable cups
récupérer l'eau de pluie pour arroser le jardin	collect rainwater for watering the garden
fermer le robinet pendant qu'on se lave les dents	turn off the tap when cleaning teeth
boire l'eau du robinet	drink tap water
prendre une douche au lieu de prendre un bain	shower instead of taking a bath
tirer la chasse d'eau moins fréquemment	flush the toilet less frequently
faire plus	do more

Had a look ☐ **Nearly there** ☐ **Nailed it** ☐

D'où vient ton tee-shirt? / Where does your T-shirt come from?

Les produits pas chers sont souvent fabriqués dans des conditions de travail inacceptables.	Cheap products are often made in unacceptable working conditions.
Les ouvriers sont sous-payés.	The workers are underpaid.
Leur journée de travail est trop longue.	Their working day is too long.
Si un produit est bon marché, je ne l'achète pas.	If a product is cheap, I don't buy it.
Trop de travailleurs sont exploités/exposés à des risques.	Too many workers are exploited/exposed to risks.

Had a look ☐ **Nearly there** ☐ **Nailed it** ☐

French	English
À mon avis, on devrait …	In my opinion, people should …
boycotter les grandes marques qui ne respectent pas leurs ouvriers	boycott big brands that don't respect their workers
forcer les grandes marques à garantir un salaire minimum	force big brands to guarantee a minimum wage
acheter des habits issus du commerce équitable	buy fairly traded clothes
acheter des vêtements fabriqués en France	buy clothes made in France

réfléchir à l'impact sur l'environnement	think about the impact on the environment
essayer de respecter l'homme et l'environnement à la fois	try to respect mankind and the environment at the same time

Had a look ☐ **Nearly there** ☐ **Nailed it** ☐

Faire du bénévolat / Volunteering

Ça me permet d'élargir mes compétences.	It allows me to expand my skills.
Ça me donne plus confiance en moi.	It gives me more confidence in myself/makes me feel more confident.
Ça me donne le sentiment d'être utile.	It makes me feel useful.
C'est important de participer à la vie en société.	It's important to participate in society.
On a la responsabilité d'aider les autres et de ne pas se focaliser sur soi-même.	We have a responsibility to help others and not focus on ourselves.
Je travaille …	I work …
sur un stand d'Oxfam	on an Oxfam stand
dans un refuge pour les animaux	in an animal sanctuary
Je fais partie de l'organisation X.	I'm a member of X.
Je rends visite à une personne âgée.	I visit an elderly person.
Je participe à des projets de conservation.	I take part in conservation projects.
J'aide des enfants du primaire à faire leurs devoirs.	I help primary school children to do their homework.
Je soigne les animaux.	I look after/treat animals.
Je soutiens les SDF.	I support homeless people.
On s'adresse aux …	We appeal to …
sensibiliser	to raise awareness
prendre conscience de	to become aware of
soigner	to look after, to treat
accueillir	to welcome
affronter	to face, to confront
soutenir	to support

Had a look ☐ **Nearly there** ☐ **Nailed it** ☐

Les grands événements / Big events

Un avantage de cet événement, c'est que …	An advantage of this event is that …
D'un côté, ça …	On the one hand, it …
En plus, ça …	What's more/Moreover, it …
met en avant la culture	promotes the culture

44

Module 8 Vocabulaire

met en avant la ville hôte	promotes the host city
crée un sentiment de fierté nationale	creates a sense of national pride
permet aux gens de passer un bon moment	allows people to have a good time
encourage la pratique du sport	encourages participation in sport
unit les gens	unites people
donne des modèles aux jeunes	gives young people role models
crée du travail	creates jobs
attire des touristes	attracts tourists

Had a look ☐ **Nearly there** ☐ **Nailed it** ☐

Cependant, …	However, …
un inconvénient, c'est que …	a disadvantage is that …
D'un autre côté, …	On the other hand, …
Par ailleurs, …	What's more, …
les ouvriers qui construisent les stades sont souvent exploités	the workers who build the stadiums are often exploited
les prix augmentent	prices rise
la ville hôte est souvent endettée après l'événement	the host city is often in debt after the event
ça laisse une empreinte carbone très importante	it leaves a major carbon footprint
J'estime/Je trouve/Je suis persuadé(e) que/qu' …	I reckon/find/am persuaded that …
il y a du pour et du contre	there are pros and cons
les festivals sont une chose positive/négative pour un pays/une région	festivals are positive/negative for a country/region
les panneaux solaires	solar panels
les toilettes sèches	dry toilets
les véhicules électriques	electric vehicles
le papier recyclé	recycled paper

Had a look ☐ **Nearly there** ☐ **Nailed it** ☐

M 8

45

Module 8 Vocabulaire

Extra words I should know for reading and listening activities

Le monde	*The world*
la pauvreté	poverty
les déchets (m)	rubbish
la surpêche	overfishing
l'empreinte carbone (f)	carbon footprint
les produits bio (m)	organic products
le covoiturage	car share
l'hébergement (m)	accommodation
l'association caritative (f)	charity organisation
les manifestations (f)	demonstrations
les pétitions (f)	petitions
les conflits (m)	conflicts
les campagnes (f)	campaigns
la sensibilisation	raising awareness
la chasse	hunting
les JO (m)	Olympic games
les habitants (m)	inhabitants
le profile	profile
les sans-abri (m)*	homeless people
l'appareil électrique (m)	electrical device
le chauffage	heating
le gobelet	tumbler
les bocaux en verre (m)	glass jars

Had a look ☐ Nearly there ☐ Nailed it ☐

Les problèmes et les solutions	*Problems and solutions*
se ficher de	to not care about something
réduire	to reduce
prendre conscience de	to become aware of
se plaindre	to complain
abandonner	to abandon
souligner	to underline

accueillir	to welcome
consacrer	to devote
faciliter	to facilitate
parrainer	to sponsor
inquiéter	to worry
agir	to act
mener	to lead
compter	to count
entreprendre	to undertake
lancer	to launch
tourner le dos à qqn	to turn your back on someone
donner le bras à qqn	to give someone a hand
offrir un café à qqn	to buy someone a coffee
donner un coup de poing à qqn	to hit someone
requis(e)	required
endetté(e)	indebted
festivalier	festival-goer
en tissu	made of material/cloth

Had a look ☐ Nearly there ☐ Nailed it ☐

Les expressions idiomatiques	*Idioms*
du coup	as a result, thus
à la fois	at the same time
en fil de fer	made of wire
en train de	in the middle of
longtemps considéré comme …	long considered as …
un milliard	a billion
des milliers**	thousands

Had a look ☐ Nearly there ☐ Nailed it ☐

---

*Sans + noun indicates a group of people who do not possess something: homes, legal documents, etc.

Examples:

Les Sans-culottes ('the without breeches') were the common people of the lower classes in late 18th century France, lots of whom fought in the French Revolution in response to their poor quality of life.

Les sans-papiers people without papers/illegal immigrants

**Look for words you know already that you see within new words, for example:

mille thousand / *milliers* thousands

ISBN 978-1-292-13243-3